The New York Times

LOOKING FORWARD

Military Spending

T0243233

THE NEW YORK TIMES EDITORIAL STAFF

Published in 2020 by New York Times Educational Publishing
in association with The Rosen Publishing Group, Inc.
29 East 21st Street, New York, NY 10010

First Edition

The New York Times
Alex Ward: Editorial Director, Book Development
Phyllis Collazo: Photo Rights/Permissions Editor
Heidi Giovine: Administrative Manager

Rosen Publishing
Megan Kellerman: Managing Editor
Greg Clinton: Editor
Greg Tucker: Creative Director
Brian Garvey: Art Director

Cataloging-in-Publication Data
Names: New York Times Company.
Title: Military spending / edited by the New York Times editorial staff.
Description: New York : New York Times Educational Publishing,
2020. | Series: Looking forward | Includes glossary and index.
Identifiers: ISBN 9781642822724 (library bound) | ISBN
9781642822717 (pbk.) | ISBN 9781642822731 (ebook)
Subjects: LCSH:United States. Department of Defense—
Appropriations and expenditures. | United States—Armed
Forces—Appropriations and expenditures.
Classification: LCC UA23.M555 2020 | DDC 355.6'220973—dc23

Manufactured in the United States of America

On the cover: In the Arabian Sea, an MH-60S Knighthawk lifts
cargo from the fast combat support ship USNS Rainier (T-AOE-7)
for vertical replenishment with the Nimitz-class aircraft carrier
USS John C. Stennis, Oct. 20, 2011; Stocktrek Images/Getty
Images.

Contents

CHAPTER 2

The Politics of Proliferation

CHAPTER 3

Private Industry

CHAPTER 4

A New Era of War and National Defense

CHAPTER 5

Case Study: The F-35 Joint Strike Fighter

Introduction

ON APRIL 4, 1967, Martin Luther King Jr. delivered a speech at Riverside Church in New York City in which he argued that the United States should not be engaged in a war in Vietnam, that the war had too many moral failings to be justified and that the fight against communism — a significant conflict for U.S. politics in the mid-20th century — would be won only through a positive appeal to justice rather than relying on armed conflict. Nearing the climax of his speech, King declared that "a nation that continues year after year to spend more money on military defense than on programs of social uplift is approaching spiritual death."

King was not initiating the opposition between military spending and social spending; the debate about allocating resources to defense or domestic issues has raged since the moment the United States was born. But he articulated a key element in the history of military proliferation: How much is enough? The question immediately gives rise to other, more complex questions, such as: With a finite federal budget, does military spending mean spending less on education and health care? Should the government spend money now to meet theoretical or speculative threats that might arise in the future? If military technology is top secret and scrutiny may reveal those secrets to adversaries, how can a democratic society effectively oversee military budgets? And if private defense technology companies make up a significant part of the military contracts to develop and build weapons, does a "war on budgets" also mean job losses and economic cuts in regions that rely on the defense industry?

An F-35B Lightning fighter jet outside a maintenance hangar between test flights at Patuxent River Naval Air Station in Patuxent, Md., April 19, 2012. The F-35 Joint Strike Fighter, still plagued by technological troubles after more than a decade of development, will ultimately cost taxpayers $396 billion if the Pentagon sticks to its plan.

Put simply, what President Dwight D. Eisenhower called "the military-industrial complex" — that loose partnership between government defense programs and private defense contractors — is enormously influential in American politics and policy, and its influence is difficult to counter given its intractable complexity. But when taxpayers agree to allow their tax contributions to fund such a lucrative trade, scrutiny is inevitable. Almost from the beginning, politicians and the general public have held military budgets in skeptical regard, suspecting that behind the veil of secrecy is an inefficient and perhaps even wasteful system. Added to this is the ironic truth that even if the system is efficient, the result of its efficiency is violence.

The articles and opinions in this book take a critical but not necessarily oppositional look at military spending in the United States, its intricacies and difficulties, its secrecy and necessity and the ways it is enmeshed in the politics and economics of the country. The recent case of the F-35 Joint Strike Fighter and its many budgetary overages highlights how complex it can be to balance the needs of defense, the temptations to profit from arms sales, the demands of taxpayers and their political representatives, and the special interests of military branches with their own incentives and goals.

CHAPTER 1

Fighting Against Waste and Inefficiency

The debate over military spending in the United States is often framed like this: On the one hand, national security concerns require research, development and manufacture of large numbers of advanced (and expensive) weapons; on the other hand, fiscal responsibility and the need to fund social programs requires military budget cuts. Attempts to audit the military and make it more efficient run into a different problem: secrecy. As the need for secret weapons increases, especially after the advent of nuclear weapons, making military budgets fully public is problematic. Nonetheless, the debate rages on, as these articles illustrate.

Pentagon Profligacy

EDITORIAL | BY THE NEW YORK TIMES | JAN. 9, 1970

WHEN SENATOR PROXMIRE of Wisconsin suggested recently that military spending could be cut by $10 billion, some members of his House-Senate Economy subcommittee scoffed. But when the subcommittee resumed its probe of Pentagon profligacy last month, Mr. Proxmire demonstrated he was not "just pulling figures out of thin air," as his critics had charged.

A General Accounting Office official told the subcommittee that the cost of 38 major weapons systems has increased by more than $20 billion, a rise of nearly 50 per cent over initial estimates. Particularly shocking was the case of a deep-diving rescue craft for the Navy. Originally to cost $36 million for twelve vessels, the bill is now put at $63 million for only six.

A civilian cost expert for the Navy told of escalating costs, misplaced equipment, delayed delivery and poor performance in a new destroyer program. Such disclosures of Pentagon waste are by no means new. Senator Proxmire helped jolt Congress into making substantial cuts in the defense budget early in 1969 with his revelations of vast overruns in the cost of the C-5A cargo planes and other major procurement items. But there still has been little effective action to reform military procurement practices.

An amendment to the defense appropriation bill that would have required regular review and reporting on defense contracts by the G.A.O. was killed in conference. One witness testified that there is still no central official or agency within the Department of Defense keeping track of weapons development. Indeed, the Pentagon has demonstrated its contempt for economy by firing A. Ernest Fitzgerald, the courageous cost expert who first exposed the C-5A overrun.

Cost overruns are not the only, or even the major source of Pentagon waste, as Senator Proxmire and others have repeatedly pointed out. Major reductions in defense spending can be made only when the President and Congress insist on eliminating Pentagon projects such as the ABM that are extravagant at any price. But it is evident from the findings of the Proxmire subcommittee that more substantial reductions in the defense budget could be achieved by thorough administrative and legislative reform of Pentagon purchasing procedures.

Cut the Military Budget? Oh, Sure

BY BILL KELLER | JAN. 14, 1985

REPRESENTATIVE WILLIAM L. DICKINSON, the top Republican on the House Armed Services Committee, had this to say about the military budget President Reagan is preparing to send Congress next month:

"I'd be embarrassed to get up and try to defend what he's proposed."

And the Alabama Congressman had this to say when pressed for one example of where the military budget should be cut:

"Listen, I've got somebody waiting to take me to lunch."

Such is the collective dilemma that confronts members of the 99th Congress.

SOMEONE HAS TO CHOOSE

They arrive with a conviction that the military must contribute more to reducing the Federal deficit. Even conservatives like Mr. Dickinson and the Senate Armed Services chairman, Barry Goldwater, say so.

There is growing enthusiasm for a "freeze" of Pentagon spending, halting the military buildup at this year's level, probably with an adjustment for inflation. But even those who support a freeze say they do not believe the military should just stop everything in its tracks for a year.

Someone, Congress or the Pentagon, eventually has to choose which programs grow and which shrink so that the total stays within the budget limits.

Missiles? Troops? Pensions? Research? Pick a category and there is an influential crowd of supporters who argue that that particular item is vital to national security, politically untouchable or otherwise off-limits.

'THIS ELABORATE DANCE'

Some advocates of lower military spending predict that after much hue and cry, 1985 will be little different from the past few years.

"We have this elaborate dance, but we end up in about the same place," said Senator Jeff Bingaman, a New Mexico Democrat who has watched the dance for two years from his seat on the Armed Services Committee. "I don't see a great deal in the equation that has changed from last year or the year before."

"Spine transplants are what we really need to take Reagan on," said Representative Patricia Schroeder, Democrat of Colorado, a military critic on the House Armed Services Committee.

In fact, Congress has managed to cut fairly deeply into President Reagan's budget requests. But it has done so without interrupting the upward trajectory of military spending or fundamentally changing the way the money is spent.

The military budget has grown a record six straight years in "real," that is, inflation-adjusted, dollars, pushing past the spending peaks of the wars in Vietnam and Korea.

RELATIVELY PAINLESS CHANGES

Much of what Congress has saved along the way has come from relatively painless changes: A 4 percent pay increase for troops instead of 5.5 percent, 440 Patriot missiles for the Army instead of 585, a decision not to reactivate an old battleship, a windfall from declining inflation and fuel costs, some better bargains extracted from contractors.

But this year Congress will get a budget with much of the easy savings squeezed out. Under pressure from the President's budget advisers to make a show of austerity, Defense Secretary Caspar W. Weinberger has already "given up" $11.1 billion in spending authority for next year, mostly through postponing pay increases and reaping the bookkeeping benefits of lower inflation.

What is left, according to military budget experts, presents Congress with some unpleasant choices.

Take weapons. Military hardware, especially nuclear arms, has been the fastest-growing account in the military budget under President Reagan. From 1980 to 1985, spending on major conventional weapons doubled and on nuclear weapons almost quadrupled.

CONSTITUENCY FOR EVERY WEAPON

Yet Congress and the military have been generally unwilling to take on the organized phalanx of contractors, service personnel and jobs-minded politicians who defend any major weapon.

"Cutting weapons is something everybody agrees to in general, but it's difficult to get a majority to agree to it in specifics," Mr. Bingaman said. "Each system has its own constituency."

Indeed, if this year is true to history, the Pentagon will send Congress a budget that slyly excludes some things it knows Congress is likely to put back: M1 tanks made in Michigan, for example, or attack submarines built in Virginia and Connecticut, or tanker planes for the ever-popular National Guard, which has an active lobby.

In addition, the big nuclear weapons like the MX missile may be helped this year by arms talks in Geneva. Defenders will argue that Congress should not force the Administration to make concessions while it is in mid-bargaining.

When Congress and the military do cut weapons spending they usually go at it by buying fewer of each weapon each year, a practice called "stretching out."

Critics like Senator Sam Nunn, the Georgia Democrat, argue that this is wasteful because it means each weapon carries more of the manufacturer's overhead and thus is produced at a higher cost.

DOLLAR CUT ISN'T A DOLLAR SAVED

Another problem with cutting weapons is that a dollar appropriated for a weapon is actually doled out over several years, as contractors deliver on their long-term contracts.

Scrapping a new weapon may make it easier to balance the books in future years (just as much of this year's military budget is committed to finishing off old commitments). But cutting that weapons dollar will reduce this year's deficit by only 15 cents.

Congress is notorious for caring more about this year's deficit than next year's.

One way to cut the deficit right now is by reducing personnel costs. A dollar of military pay goes straight into a paycheck.

Mr. Weinberger, with his eye on the immediate deficit, proposed last month to delay a pay raise for the men and women in uniform and to cut the pay of the Pentagon's one million civilian employees.

But Mr. Dickinson and others say Congress is unlikely to cut any deeper into pay and may restore some of the savings claimed by Mr. Weinberger.

One of the military's proudest accomplishments in the past few years has been recruiting legions of qualified soldiers into the volunteer Army. Now there are signs that this success is threatened by a decline in the numbers of potential recruits and competition from the growing civilian economy.

"I think we've got to be very clear that we're not getting into those quality-of-life programs," said Representative Joseph M. McDade of Pennsylvania, the top Republican on the House military spending subcommittee, referring to the pay and pensions credited with helping lure new recruits. "If we have a success story, that is it."

For similar reasons, Congress has grown leery of cutting other aspects of "combat readiness," such as training, ammunition stocks, spare parts and flying hours. Once these were fair game for nibbling away at the budget, but not since press reports that many combat units are ill-prepared to fight.

IN SEARCH OF FAT

There is, of course, one category Congress could cut by acclamation. Waste.

Inflamed by reports of misfiring missiles and $7,600 coffeemakers, Congress has been pressuring the Pentagon to reform its buying habits, with mixed results.

The problem is that fat, when it exists, is usually well marbled through the budget, not sitting on top awaiting the carving knife.

As Representative Les Aspin of Wisconsin, the new chairman of the House Armed Services Committee, once put it: "There is no line item in the budget that says: 'Waste, fraud and abuse — $8,924,673,749.34.' "

Pentagon Struggles With Cost Overruns and Delays

BY LESLIE WAYNE | JULY 11, 2006

ON SEPT. 10, 2001, Defense Secretary Donald H. Rumsfeld stood before hundreds of military officers and civilian employees at the Pentagon and delivered a blistering attack on what he saw as the next national security threat: Pentagon bureaucracy.

He called for quicker decision-making, greater accountability and a streamlined process to get weapons into the hands of soldiers faster. "We must transform the way the department works and what it works on," he said. "It could be said that it's a matter of life and death — ultimately, every American's."

The terrorist attacks the next day did more than put Mr. Rumsfeld's transformation plans in suspension. As new weapons systems were ordered to help fight the war on terror, Pentagon spending after 9/11 jumped by hundreds of billions of dollars. And so did waste.

Now, almost five years later, Congress has promised to clamp down on the inefficiencies and wasteful practices that Mr. Rumsfeld identified, which critics and government oversight agencies say have only grown worse with the flood of new money into military spending.

Members of Congress from both parties are concerned that runaway costs threaten to weaken the armed forces as higher price tags mean they can afford fewer weapons.

In the current Pentagon budget for 2007, steps have been taken to, among other things, require fuller disclosure of cost overruns, set spending caps and use more fixed-price contracts that require contractors to stay within budget. Senator John McCain, Republican of Arizona and chairman of a Senate Armed Services subcommittee, plans to hold hearings this summer and next year on the issue.

Cost overruns have long been a Pentagon staple. But what has alarmed government oversight agencies and Pentagon observers, and spurred Congress to act, is the magnitude of the spending increases. Projects are as much as 50 percent over budget and up to four years late in delivery.

"We have been living in a rich man's world for the last five years," said Jacques Gansler, Pentagon under secretary for acquisition from 1997 to 2001 and vice president for research at the University of Maryland. "The defense budget has been growing so rapidly that we are less likely to put in many cost-sensitive reforms."

In recent Congressional hearings and reports from the Government Accountability Office, Congress's investigative arm, the Pentagon has been portrayed as so mired in bureaucracy and so enamored of the latest high-tech gadgetry that multi-billion-dollar weapon systems are running years behind in development and are dangerously over budget.

The Pentagon reported last April, in response to questions from lawmakers, that 36 of its major next-generation weapon systems are over budget, some by as much as 50 percent.

The G.A.O. estimated that cost overruns on 23 weapon systems it studied in April came to $23 billion. In addition, there were delays of at least a year in delivering these weapons, with some programs running as much as four years late, like the Army's $130 billion Future Combat Systems to provide soldiers new computerized ground equipment.

David Walker, comptroller general of the United States, said in testimony before the House Armed Services Committee last April that "the Department of Defense is simply not positioned to deliver high-quality products in a timely and cost-efficient fashion."

Rising costs can also mean that fewer weapons are ultimately built. For instance, the budget for a military rocket launching program, the Evolved Expendable Launch Vehicle, has increased from $15.4 billion to $28 billion. Even so, the program is anticipating fewer launchings: 138 instead of the 181 initially planned.

Costs for an information-gathering satellite program, called the Space-Based Infrared System, have grown from $4.1 billion to $10.2

billion. Meanwhile, the number of satellites has decreased from five to three.

"It's a perfect storm," said Lawrence J. Korb, a former Pentagon assistant secretary, who served in the Reagan administration and is now a senior fellow at the Center for American Progress. "You had this big buildup in military spending. That took a bubbling problem and made it worse. It made it more difficult to audit and keep track of what was going on. It's always been bad, but I've never seen it this bad."

Blame for the cost overruns is not easily assigned. Even though Mr. Rumsfeld identified the Pentagon itself as a problem in early 2001, the rapid buildup and cost overruns in recent years resulted from widespread calls for more military might.

While Mr. Rumsfeld has been successful in getting a few outmoded weapons systems deleted — his main triumphs have been killing the $11 billion Crusader artillery program and the $38 billion Comanche helicopter program — any momentum he developed for Pentagon transformation was overtaken by his focus on Iraq.

"Clearly, since 9/11, transformation has not been a focus of Rumsfeld," Mr. Korb said.

WAR EXPENSES ADD TO PRESSURE

These cost overruns come as the Pentagon is under pressure on two fronts. It is trying to get weapons to soldiers in Iraq while embarking on a complex new procurement program costing hundreds of billions of dollars.

The Pentagon wants to fundamentally transform the military with more lethal and technologically superior "megasystems." The Navy is spending $80 billion for advanced submarines and $70 billion for destroyers. The Air Force is in the midst of a $320 billion program to recapitalize its fighter jet fleet and the Army has ordered $130 billion in computerized replacements for tanks and other vehicles.

With numbers this large, even slight delays and overruns can quickly become billion-dollar problems.

Meantime, the Bush administration has warned the Pentagon that the current high level of military spending cannot be sustained, raising new questions of whether the Pentagon can afford everything it has committed to — or in the numbers it wants.

Some in Congress say the prospect of paying more for fewer weapons is, in itself, a kind of threat to national security. "Acquisition inefficiencies may, in the end, drive American vulnerabilities more than any other dimension of America's national security complex," said Representative Duncan Hunter, the California Republican who is chairman of the House Armed Services Committee.

The Pentagon says it is fully aware of these problems and is moving to correct them.

"We've got a lot of traction in the building, and I'm coming to help harness that traction and take it to the end zone," said James I. Finley, under secretary for acquisition.

Mr. Finley, a former General Dynamics executive, is working to speed Pentagon decision-making, make the high-tech requirements for new weapons more realistic, and reduce the numerous design changes ordered by the Pentagon.

The impact on the Pentagon's budget from the overruns is hard to gauge. That is because simply determining how much money the Pentagon has is difficult, the G.A.O. said last year.

The recordkeeping is so flawed and lacking in basic financial controls that government auditors are unable to provide a "clean" or conclusive opinion under basic accounting rules.

The G.A.O. found that financial sloppiness went beyond weapon systems. For instance, at a time when the Pentagon was buying new chemical suits for use in Iraq for $200 each, it was also selling them on the Internet for $3 each after some military units misidentified the suits as surplus. And about $1.2 billion in supplies that were shipped to Iraq never arrived — or were never found — because of logistical problems.

But the really big money is in weapons. New weapons are expected to cost at least $1.4 trillion from now to 2009, with $800 billion of those expenditures yet to be made, according to the Pentagon. Weapons systems are one of the largest purchases made by the federal government, and the Pentagon's weapons-buying program has doubled from $700 billion before 9/11.

Since 9/11, the Pentagon budget and supplemental spending on Iraq have grown to over $500 billion a year. This compares with a Pentagon budget of $291 billion before 9/11. (If measured in today's dollars, pre-9/11 spending would come to $330 billion, according to the Pentagon.)

A number of Pentagon improvement efforts — Mr. Rumsfeld's best known is called the Business Management Modernization Program — have been tried in the last five years, to little effect. This shortcoming has not gone unnoticed in business circles.

A group called Business Leaders for Sensible Priorities, which includes 600 executives from companies like Bell Industries, the Pacific Stock Exchange and the Stride Rite Corporation, issued a report on Pentagon financial practices last May called "No One Is Accountable."

It concluded: "The Defense Department's financial management practices would put any civilian company out of business."

A MOVE TOWARD MORE CONTROL

In the last few months, Congress has moved to assert more control. In the House, Mr. Hunter put provisions in the Pentagon budget requiring more reporting on overruns, allowing for the rebidding of contracts with exceptional overruns and imposing spending caps on some weapons.

In the Senate, the Armed Services Committee has enacted provisions calling for more fixed-price weapons contracts, limiting award fees to contractors and providing for more Congressional oversight of prime contractors on major programs.

The Pentagon's finances are under increasing scrutiny because the Bush administration has indicated that Pentagon budgets will begin to flatten in 2008. In addition, annual supplemental funding of $100 billion for Iraq and Afghanistan is expected to go away, with the funds to come instead from the Pentagon budget.

A federal budget deficit remaining around $300 billion and the rising demands to support entitlement programs as society ages also mean the Pentagon will have to compete harder for dollars. Inside the Pentagon, the growing gap between available resources and future demands is called the bow wave: a surge of costs that threatens to swamp the Pentagon just as military budgets begin to decline.

Military contractors are aware of these problems, but have little incentive to address them. Critics say contractors fail to object to the Pentagon's business practices since the industry is paid regardless of the outcome. The industry says its hands are tied.

"This industry is rather unique," said Norman R. Augustine, a former chief executive of Lockheed Martin Corporation and a former Army under secretary. "It has only one customer, but it is the most powerful customer in the world. It makes and enforces the rules, and if you want to do business with that customer, you do what that customer wants.

"Where the big money is lost," he added, "is in starting programs and stopping, cutting the budget and then raising it, slowing and then accelerating programs, setting requirements and then revising them."

Instead, Mr. Augustine said, "what is needed most is to make it extremely difficult to start a new program" and not until "the need is clear, the technology is there and there is money to do the job."

Critics say the solution is not more money, but a different approach. The Pentagon, they say, is unable to separate wants from needs and approves far more than it can afford.

The Pentagon then sets technical requirements unrealistically high and compounds this problem by trying to rush weapon systems with unproven technologies into production. Rather than producing weapons faster, the opposite effect occurs, as the inevitable technological difficulties lead to cost overruns and developmental delays. In addition, once weapons programs are started, the Pentagon often imposes new requirements, adding further delays and costs.

Frequent turnover in program managers at the Pentagon, as well as a lack of either responsibility or accountability by officials for specific weapons programs, means there are few consequences when programs go astray, the G.A.O. said. It added that lack of accountability can extend to contractors as well.

In the civilian world, development costs are borne by companies themselves. Boeing, for instance, must absorb all the costs of developing a new line of commercial jets before selling them. But pay starts for military contractors even during development of new weapons, and the contractors do not face market forces to get weapons quickly to their customer, the Pentagon.

Nor are contractors held accountable when they underperform. A G.A.O. study in December found that the Pentagon had paid $8 billion in bonus award fees to military contractors regardless of whether performance goals were met.

For instance, contractors on the Joint Strike Fighter, a next-generation fighter jet, received their full bonus award of $494 million from 1999 to 2003, even though the program was $10 billion over budget and 11 months behind schedule.

Contractors in the F-22A fighter jet program, over the same time period, received 91 percent of their performance bonus, or $849 million, even though the current phase of the program was $10 billion over budget and two years late.

Mr. Walker, the comptroller general, said in testimony before the House Armed Services Committee that the Pentagon needed to make it "clear who is responsible for what and holding people accountable when these responsibilities are not fulfilled."

The biggest program in the Pentagon pipeline is the Air Force's replacement of its tactical aircraft fleet, primarily F-16's, with F-22A's and the Joint Strike Fighter. The combined price tag for the replacement plan is $320 billion, with $75 billion of that already appropriated. But problems are already cropping up from what critics say is a "conspiracy of hope" rather than hard-edged planning.

One consequence of rising costs is that about 4,500 F-16's and other jets will be replaced by only 3,100 new jets. And as the Air Force waits for its new jets, it has stopped buying F-16's. This means the newest models are flown by the United Arab Emirates and Poland, which have recently placed large orders.

When it was planned 19 years ago, the F-22A was an ambitious project by any measure. It was to fly invisibly, at supersonic speeds and with the latest in avionics and engines. All this was to counter Soviet threats in air-to-air combat. Initially, the Air Force had planned to spend $82 billion and buy 648 planes.

Since then, the Soviet threat ended and the F-22A encountered numerous cost overruns and schedule delays. The Air Force also added new requirements so the jet could also conduct bombing missions — even though some critics question the feasibility of using an expensive fighter jet that flies at nearly twice the speed of sound to attack ground targets.

In the end, the F-22A is costing nearly twice as much per plane as planned, and the Air Force is getting only one-quarter the number it had initially sought. The cost for each plane has soared to $361 million, making it the most expensive fighter jet ever. It is still not ready for combat.

FEWER PLANES FOR MORE MONEY

The Air Force maintains it needs at least 381 F-22A's to satisfy national security requirements. But the Pentagon has only enough money to buy 181, leaving a shortfall of about 200 aircraft. By contrast, the F-16 fighter jet began as a less ambitious program and was built in four years, using proven technology. It has been flying, with continual upgrades, for 30 years and is considered the most successful fighter jet in history.

Many in Congress are concerned that the replacement for the F-16, the Joint Strike Fighter being developed under a $257 billion program, may not be as cost-effective. Development costs have already risen by $23 billion, or 28 percent. This has caused the Pentagon to cut 400 planes from the program, which is now set for 2,443 planes.

Equally troublesome to critics is that the Pentagon has invested in manufacturing and producing the plane before it has been fully tested. The G.A.O. reports that when initial production of the Joint Strike Fighter begins next January, only 1 percent of its preflight testing will be completed. Longtime Pentagon watchers say that optimism about weapons and budgets is part of its inherent character. But the reality of limited funds and a growing chorus of critics may ultimately force the gap to close between what the Pentagon wants and what it can afford.

"We've always wanted to provide the best for our boys and we have been willing to pay for it," said Mr. Gansler, the former acquisitions under secretary. "The belief has been that next year we will be richer and the budget will climb even more. But now, as the Pentagon has to be more cost sensitive, you have to question the belief."

$296 Billion in Overruns in U.S. Weapons Programs

BY CHRISTOPHER DREW | MARCH 30, 2009

NEARLY 70 PERCENT of the Pentagon's 96 largest weapons programs were over budget last year, for a combined total of $296 billion more than the original estimates, a Congressional auditing agency reported Monday.

The findings, compiled by the Government Accountability Office, seemed likely to add to the pressure on officials to make sizable cuts in the most troubled programs as they work out the details of a proposed $664 billion defense budget for fiscal 2010.

President Obama has said that the "days of giving defense contractors a blank check are over." Pentagon officials have said they will finish putting together a list of proposed cuts in April.

In a letter to Congress, Gene L. Dodaro, the acting comptroller general for the G.A.O., an auditing agency, said that while there had been modest improvements in the last year, the Pentagon's management of the contracts remained poor, and cost overruns were "still staggering."

The accountability office reported that the programs were behind schedule by an average of 22 months, up from 21 months last year and 18 months in 2003.

The office had previously said that the cost of a similar portfolio of programs had risen by $295 billion through 2007, or $301 billion when adjusted for inflation.

In the report released on Monday, the G.A.O. said the Pentagon often had to reduce the number of planes and ships it could buy.

The report said, for instance, that the cost of 10 of the largest weapons systems was running 32 percent higher than projected, and the quantities that could be purchased had been cut.

Some programs, like the Air Force's F-22 fighter jet and the Army's Future Combat System, are among the systems that Defense Secretary Robert M. Gates has said he is scrutinizing.

According to the G.A.O., the F-22, which was designed in the 1980s, was originally expected to cost $88 billion in 2009 dollars for 648 planes. The program is now expected to cost $73.7 billion for the 184 planes.

Some military analysts say they believe that Mr. Gates will recommend canceling the plane, or buying fewer planes than the Air Force wants.

But the G.A.O. also said the Pentagon had done a better job of managing some newer programs.

In a response to the office, John J. Young Jr., the Pentagon's top acquisition official, said department officials had "instituted several major changes that are beginning to show results."

Mr. Young also noted that in some cases, the cost growth was not a result of overruns but of program expansions. And in others, delays were ordered by top Pentagon officials or Congress as part of budgeting trade-offs.

Military Costs Under Review in Bid to Trim Waste

BY CHRISTOPHER DREW | JUNE 27, 2010

THE PENTAGON'S EFFORT to cut more than $100 billion in administrative costs over the next several years is expected to take a new direction on Monday with proposals that could lower profits for military companies.

Industry officials said that Ashton B. Carter, the under secretary of defense for acquisition, had called a meeting with contractors and lobbyists to address ways to cut waste. In addition to trimming its own bureaucracy, the Pentagon is looking for savings in how it hands out hundreds of billions of dollars in contracts for weapons and services each year.

Mr. Carter is expected to question overhead costs built into many deals and the amount of profit on certain types of contracts, the industry officials said. Congressional auditors have long criticized the Pentagon for awarding too many contracts in which it covers all the costs and pays sizable fees even when companies have trouble performing.

At the major military companies, "everyone's apprehensive" about the meeting, said Loren B. Thompson, the chief operating officer of the Lexington Institute, a research group financed in part by the contractors.

"They're worried about the tangible impact on profits," he said. "But they're also worried about the atmospherics that are conveyed to Wall Street and how investors will react."

Cheryl Irwin, a Pentagon spokeswoman, said Sunday that Mr. Carter did not want to comment publicly in advance of the meeting.

The meeting stems from a larger push by the defense secretary, Robert M. Gates, to free up money for troops in the field. But any efforts to cut costs involving contractors could signal a downturn for the industry, which has had record profits since military spending soared after the 9/11 terrorist attacks.

Even though Mr. Gates canceled a number of prominent weapons programs last year, the department's budgets have continued to rise under President Obama, to $708 billion proposed for next year, including the costs of the Iraq and Afghanistan wars.

Mr. Gates has said he would like to see the Pentagon's base budget, excluding the war costs, grow each year by 1 to 2 percent after inflation.

But health care and other personnel costs are taking up a rising share of the total, and many analysts doubt that the government will be able to sustain such increases as the nation's overall budget deficits expand.

Mr. Thompson, who is also a consultant to several military companies, said he believed that Mr. Carter wanted to get the industry's reaction before deciding on some of the contracting changes.

Congressional auditors have especially criticized many of the contracts for supplies and services in the war zones as being poorly drawn by the government.

They also have questioned whether the Pentagon's contracting officers have the skills and the experience to ride herd on some of the contractors. The Pentagon sharply reduced its contracting staff during the 1990s, and the Obama administration is hiring 20,000 more people.

Costly Aircraft Suggests Cuts Won't Be Easy

BY ELISABETH BUMILLER | NOV. 19, 2011

WASHINGTON — Defense Secretary Leon E. Panetta shoved his head into a snug aviator helmet topped with goggles one September morning and swooped into Lower Manhattan on a V-22 Osprey, a $70 million aircraft that Marines use for battlefield assaults in Afghanistan.

"How'd you like that gizmo?" Mr. Panetta said after landing at the Wall Street heliport in the Osprey, which takes off like a helicopter, flies like an airplane — and has been responsible for the deaths of 30 people in test flights.

Defense Department officials say the hybrid aircraft was the fastest way to get Mr. Panetta and his entourage to New York that day. But anyone who has followed the tortured history of the Osprey over the past quarter-century saw the persistent, politically savvy hand of the Marines in arranging Mr. Panetta's flight — and another example in what has become a case study of how hard it is to kill billion-dollar Pentagon programs.

"At a car dealership, what the salesman wants to do is get you inside the vehicle," said Dakota Wood, a retired Marine lieutenant colonel and defense analyst. "You take the test drive and wow, it's got a great stereo, it feels good, it has that new-car smell."

That flight with Mr. Panetta, he said, is "an insurance policy against future defense cuts."

As a joint Congressional committee appears paralyzed days from a deadline to agree on a plan to cut the nation's deficit, the Pentagon remains vulnerable to forced reductions over the next decade that would slash its spending by $500 billion, on top of $450 billion in cuts already in the works — a total of more than 15 percent of its operating budget.

But as Mr. Panetta considers scaling back major weapons programs, the Osprey illustrates the challenges in downsizing the world's most expensive military. The aircraft has survived after repeated safety problems during testing, years of delays, ballooning costs and tough questions about its utility.

Even Dick Cheney, when he was the defense secretary under the first President George Bush, could not kill it.

"Don't bet against the Marines as budget warriors," said Richard L. Aboulafia, an aviation analyst at the Teal Group in Fairfax, Va.

In just the last few weeks, the commandant of the Marine Corps, Gen. James F. Amos, has talked up the Osprey at the Council on Foreign Relations and in written testimony to Congress, branding the aircraft "revolutionary" and the arguments of its critics ill informed. The contractors who built the aircraft have been running advertisements in defense industry and news publications in Washington, celebrating its 100,000 flight hours and lauding it as the "safest Marine rotorcraft" of the last 10 years. Reporters have been flown on Osprey media flights, including with Mr. Panetta to New York.

One of the Osprey's biggest defenders on Capitol Hill, Representative William M. Thornberry, Republican of Texas (the aircraft is assembled in his district), said in a recent interview that the Osprey was much improved and "not where it was 5 or 10 years ago." Mr. Thornberry also said that one of the Osprey's biggest critics in Congress, Representative Lynn Woolsey, Democrat of California, "doesn't have a clue what she's talking about."

Mr. Thornberry was referring to Ms. Woolsey's comments on the House floor in May, when she called the Osprey "a poster child for the excesses and inefficiencies of the military-industrial complex" and offered an amendment to kill its financing. The measure failed, but an aide to Ms. Woolsey said she remained steadfast in her opposition.

Defense industry analysts say that the number of Ospreys could well be cut back from the 458 expected to be bought by the Marines, the Navy and the Air Force, but that the program is so far along it is unlikely the Pentagon or Congress will kill it entirely. (The far bigger target is the F-35 Joint Strike Fighter, the most expensive weapons

The V-22 Osprey, a $70 million craft made by Bell Helicopter Textron and Boeing, takes off like a helicopter and flies like a plane.

program in history, although the Pentagon press secretary, George Little, reiterated Saturday that "no decisions have been made" about reductions in any weapons programs.) But at this point nearly 300 Ospreys are already in service or in production, and some $36 billion out of a projected $54 billion has been spent.

"We've gone this far, we may as well make the most of it," said Mr. Aboulafia, who said the Osprey had overcome its earlier problems and was a "good aircraft," although costly.

He credited the contractors, Bell Helicopter Textron and Boeing, but particularly the Marines, for a relentless lobbying and public relations campaign.

That campaign spanned 25 years and went into overdrive when Mr. Cheney, under orders from the first President Bush to cut spending, tried to cancel the Osprey. He said it was too expensive (at the time, the projection was $28 billion for 682 aircraft) for what he viewed as the Marines' relatively narrow mission, amphibious assault.

But the Marines saw the aircraft as crucial to their survival as a quick-response, expeditionary force. In arguments they still make today, the Marines pressed their case that the Osprey could take off from aircraft carriers and get in and out of difficult landing zones better than airplanes and faster than helicopters, carry more people and save lives. In response to Mr. Cheney, they led a fierce counterattack, meeting with lobbyists and supporters in Congress in secret strategy sessions on Capitol Hill.

"It bordered on insubordination that the Marines conducted themselves the way they did," said Richard Whittle, the author of the definitive book about the program, "The Dream Machine: The Untold History of the Notorious V-22 Osprey."

"The secretary of defense had said, 'We're killing this program,' " Mr. Whittle said, "and the Marines were plotting behind the scenes with his opponents."

Led by Textron lobbyists and Curt Weldon, then a Republican representative from Pennsylvania whose district included a Boeing helicopter plant where the vehicle's fuselage was built, the group briefed members of Congress about the jobs the Osprey would bring to their districts, offered Congressional trips to Osprey factories, held Osprey lunches, pushed for Osprey hearings and organized a pro-Osprey coalition of business leaders.

"We pulled out all the stops," Mr. Weldon recalled in a recent interview. The Marines now say the aircraft survived on its merits, not because they took on Capitol Hill. But their campaign was a near-legend in the industry — and could be invoked in the military budget battles to come.

Mr. Cheney eventually admitted defeat, and the Osprey endured even through its test crashes and groundings in the 1990s. By 2007 it finally went into service, in Iraq, where Lt. Gen. John F. Kelly, then the commander of the Marines in Anbar Province, oversaw the first two squadrons of Ospreys in combat. The speed of the aircraft "turned a province the size of Texas into Rhode Island," he recalled.

General Kelly is now Mr. Panetta's senior military assistant, and it was his idea to fly the boss to New York by Osprey. Although General Kelly is an Osprey enthusiast, he insisted that his goal was not to sell Mr. Panetta on the aircraft, but to solve the logistical issue of getting him to the Sept. 11 memorials in Manhattan and Shanksville, Pa., and back to Washington in one day. It was too far for a helicopter, and taking a plane would have required too much time for ground transport.

"The only real way to do it was in Ospreys," General Kelly said.

Not that Mr. Panetta was initially enthusiastic. "He, like everybody, has this thing in his mind — 'Oh, this is this death trap,' " General Kelly said. But Mr. Panetta, who got a splendid view from the jump seat between the Osprey's two pilots, "loved it," the general said.

It did not hurt that one of the pilots had flown an Osprey that rescued a downed American pilot in Libya in March and kept the defense secretary transfixed with stories from the front.

The Libya rescue was one of the aircraft's recent successes, but an Air Force Osprey crashed in Afghanistan last year, killing 4 of the 22 aboard, with a specific cause not determined. The previous defense secretary, Robert M. Gates, flew on Ospreys too, although in the craft's more natural habitat in Afghanistan. In 2008 as a presidential candidate, Barack Obama flew on one in Iraq.

No one knows what, if anything, Mr. Panetta will decide about the V-22 as he pores over the Pentagon's books. But Defense Department officials say he is still talking about his ride. As he told reporters that day: "Interesting way to fly."

Cuts Give Obama Path to Create Leaner Military

BY DAVID E. SANGER AND THOM SHANKER | MARCH 10, 2013

WASHINGTON — At a time when $46 billion in mandatory budget cuts are causing anxiety at the Pentagon, administration officials see one potential benefit: there may be an opening to argue for deep reductions in programs long in President Obama's sights, and long resisted by Congress.

On the list are not only base closings but also an additional reduction in deployed nuclear weapons and stockpiles and a restructuring of the military medical insurance program that costs more than America spends on all of its diplomacy and foreign aid around the world. Also being considered is yet another scaling back in next-generation warplanes, starting with the F-35, the most expensive weapons program in United States history.

None of those programs would go away. But inside the Pentagon, even some senior officers are saying that the reductions, if done smartly, could easily exceed those mandated by sequestration, as the cuts are called, and leave room for the areas where the administration believes more money will be required.

These include building drones, developing offensive and defensive cyberweapons and focusing on Special Operations forces.

Publicly, at least, Mr. Obama has not backed any of those cuts, even though he has deplored the "dumb" approach of simply cutting every program in the military equally.

Mr. Obama will visit Capitol Hill on Tuesday in another attempt to persuade lawmakers to reach a long-term deficit-reduction deal and replace the indiscriminate cuts with more targeted ones.

Still, Pentagon officials are starting to examine targeted ways to cut their budget. "What we've learned in the past year is that the politics of dumb cuts is easy, because no one has to think through the implications of slicing everything by 8 percent," said one senior defense official who has been deeply involved in the planning process. "The politics of cutting individual programs is as hard as it's always been."

When Mr. Obama took office four years ago, with the Iraq and Afghanistan wars raging, deep cuts in the defense budget seemed unthinkable. He forced the Pentagon to cut nearly $50 billion a year, which was regarded by many as huge.

But today, deficit hawks outnumber defense hawks on Capitol Hill, and the possibility of $100 billion or more in additional annual cuts does not seem outrageous — if only agreement were possible on which programs should shrink fastest.

Last week, a group of five former deputy defense secretaries — essentially the Pentagon's chief operating officers — called for a "bottom up" review that reassesses the need for each major program and weapons system, saying this was an opportunity to accomplish cuts that have long been delayed, after a decade in which the American national security budget has nearly doubled.

In their more candid moments — almost always when speaking with a guarantee of anonymity — the Pentagon's top civilian and military leaders acknowledge that the painful sequestration process may ultimately prove beneficial if it forces the Defense Department and Congress to reconsider the cost of cold-war-era systems that are still in inventory despite the many changes made to the military in the last 10 years.

"Sequester is an ugly experience, but it could grow up to be a budget discipline swan," said Gordon Adams, a former senior budget official in the Clinton administration who is now at the Stimson Center, which studies defense issues. "It could provide the planning discipline the services and the building have been missing since 2001."

The central challenge facing the Pentagon and the White House, Mr. Adams and several current senior officials said, is this: All the big, immediate budget benefits come from reducing the size of active-duty forces. By contrast, cutting new weapons systems and bases and reducing health care costs can save large amounts 5 to 10 years out, but it does little in the short term.

Mr. Obama took a step in that direction in 2011, when he rejected a Pentagon request for a permanent standing force of 100,000 or so troops for future "contingency operations" like those in Iraq and Afghanistan. "That's not the way we are going to go," he told his staff after the request was received.

The message quickly got back to the Pentagon that Mr. Obama had no interest in repeating the kind of lengthy interventions that have consumed more than $3 trillion since the attacks of Sept. 11, 2001.

But the Pentagon's subsequent agreement to cut $500 billion in planned spending over a decade turns out to have been just a start, and military officials are now abandoning the phrase that they will have to "do more with less" and starting to assess what it would mean to just do less.

Toward that end, officials say that Ashton B. Carter, the deputy defense secretary, plans to convene a panel of experts to conduct a crash review of the current national military strategy with an eye to reshaping it to fit the new budget constraints.

Mr. Carter, whom the White House asked to remain under the new defense secretary, Chuck Hagel, has already cut the budget for information technology, to force the Pentagon to find cheaper ways to provide it, officials say.

But the next set of cuts will be much harder, because they involve huge constituencies — in Congressional districts, inside the military services and among veterans' groups.

"The problem is that the biggest, most-needed cuts are in programs that also have the broadest set of defenders," said Maren Leed, the director of the defense policy studies group at the Center for Strategic and International Studies in Washington and a former top aide to Gen. Ray Odierno, now the Army's chief of staff.

The most obvious examples of those problems come in base closings and higher co-payments or premiums for the beneficiaries of

Tricare, the military's sprawling health care program, which costs upward of $51 billion a year. To take the politics out of base closings, Congress in the past has established a commission to identify underused facilities, creating a list that it could either vote up or down on but could not amend.

But with many of the targeted bases now fairly obvious to members of Congress, they are reluctant even to establish a new commission. Similarly, Congress turned back a modest administration effort to revamp Tricare. "There's not a single district without a lot of beneficiaries of the system," Ms. Leed said.

Cuts in the nuclear arsenal face a different political imperative. Mr. Obama has been sitting for months on a proposal, agreed to by the Joint Chiefs of Staff, that could trim the number of active nuclear weapons in America's arsenal by nearly a third and make big cuts in the stockpile of backup weapons. But he has not signed off on it.

Rather than act unilaterally, the administration is hoping it can negotiate similar cuts with President Vladimir V. Putin of Russia — and do it without a treaty that would surely set off another battle with defense hawks in the Senate. But that prospect is doubtful, senior officials say.

Even if Mr. Obama wins his strategic argument that the arsenal is far too large for America's future defense needs, it is not clear how big the savings would be. The easiest weapons to cut — those based in silos in the middle of the country — are also the cheapest to keep in the field.

The most expensive nuclear weapons to operate are carried aboard submarines; they are also the most invulnerable to attack, and thus Pentagon and White House strategists want to preserve them the longest.

Moreover, operating a production base for nuclear weapons, the Defense Department's insurance policy in case the country ever needed to produce more, is very costly — though the administration is looking for ways to cut an $80 billion commitment to remake America's nuclear laboratories.

The biggest target of all is the F-35 Joint Strike Fighter, a new jet for the Navy, the Air Force and the Marines, and the largest single line item in the Pentagon's budget. Between $55 billion and $84 billion has already been spent, but the estimates of final production costs run close to $400 billion.

The Marine Corps says it has no choice but to go forward with its version of the plane, because its current aircraft are obsolete, and the Air Force wants to replace aging F-16s with the new, stealthy plane.

But the program was wildly mismanaged during the Bush administration — "The Joint Strike Fighter program has been both a scandal and a tragedy," Senator John McCain, Republican of Arizona, said in December 2011 — and now that the number of planes scheduled for production has already been slashed, the per-plane cost has risen to about $137 million each.

The handling of the production by Lockheed Martin, and the huge changes demanded by each of the services, has made the plane an easy target for critics.

But Lockheed has spread production over nearly every state in the union, in order to keep Congressional support high: as soon as the discussion veers toward strategic needs, Lockheed begins to stress the jobs at risk if the program were cut or canceled.

Military Is Asked to March to a Less Expensive Tune

BY DAVE PHILIPPS | JULY 1, 2016

AS FAR BACK as the Revolutionary War, the United States military has trumpeted its gleaming, brassy bands as a point of pride and a critical soft power weapon in its arsenal. But in an era of budget cuts and troop reductions, Congress is signaling that it may be time for one of the largest employers of musicians in the world to turn the music down.

The Pentagon fields more than 130 military bands worldwide, made up of about 6,500 musicians, and not just in traditional brass and drum corps like the kind that will march in many Fourth of July parades on Monday. There are also military rock acts with artsy names, conservatory-trained military jazz ensembles, military bluegrass pickers, even a military calypso band based in the Virgin Islands.

All of this cost about $437 million last year — almost three times the budget of the National Endowment for the Arts.

In June, the House of Representatives passed bills that would force the military to give a detailed accounting of the bands' activities and expenses and limit where and when the bands could perform. The House Armed Services Committee inserted a line in the latest National Defense Authorization Act saying the committee "believes that the services may be able to conserve end strength by reducing the number of military bands."

Representative Martha E. McSally, Republican of Arizona, a former Air Force fighter pilot who introduced one of the measures, noted that spending on bands had steadily increased in recent years, with the military buying $11,000 flutes and $12,000 tubas, while at the same time the Air Force has been facing a shortage of fighter pilots and aircraft maintainers.

Chief Warrant Officer Three Jeremiah Keillor directed the U.S. Army Blues, a jazz ensemble that is a part of the United States Army Band, during a military pageant at Fort Myer, Va., on Wednesday.

"While our communities certainly do enjoy being entertained by our military bands," Ms. McSally said on the House floor in June, "they would, I think, prefer to be protected by our military."

The military has staunchly defended its bands, saying music is an important asset that helps strengthen relationships with allies and bolster morale among troops. Senior leaders and enlisted musicians say bands are a relative bargain for the peace and good will they spread. Getting in requires the push-ups and shooting practice of basic training and an audition that can draw graduates of some of the country's finest music schools.

There is ample history behind military music making. At the start of the Revolutionary War, George Washington, who dabbled in the flute, personally directed the creation of a fife and drum corps and ordered that the fifes be sorted by pitch to ensure proper sound.

Staff Sgt. George Waltemire tuned his guitar between sets at Fort Myer. In addition to jazz ensembles, the military has bluegrass pickers, rock bands and even a calypso band.

"Until you see what we do, it's hard to really understand the mission impact music can have," Senior Master Sgt. Ryan Carson said in a phone interview from Doha, Qatar, where his Air Force rock band, Max Impact, is deployed.

In recent months, he and his five band mates have played in Egypt, Jordan, Kuwait and a number of what he called "undisclosed locations," performing popular songs in Arabic for foreign dignitaries, troops and children, as well as globally recognized American rock anthems by groups like Journey and Bon Jovi.

"We are allowing people to relax, connect, have meaningful interactions. For a lot of these people, it leaves a really lasting, positive impression of our country and our military," he said. "It's hard to put a value on that."

None in Congress have indicated they want to silence bands completely. Instead, they have focused on what they describe as frivolous gigs and costs that have grown considerably, even as overall military spending has shrunk.

Some military bands travel to music competitions far from relevant audiences. Others play free at festivals that charge admission. In 26 years in the Air Force, Ms. McSally said she saw plenty of performances that did nothing to further national interests. Often ensembles would play for officers at private gatherings. When she was a cadet at the Air Force Academy, the academy's band, made up of professional musicians, not cadets, played each day as students marched to lunch.

"Doing that stuff in this day and age, when we don't have enough people for combat positions?" she said in a phone interview. "I just don't get it."

Her amendment would prevent military bands from playing at many social events, including those that are not free and open to the public.

It is the latest of a number of attempts to rein in spending on bands in recent years. The first was in 2011, when Representative Betty McCollum, a Minnesota Democrat, proposed a $200 million cap on what was then a $325 million program.

"The original mission had sprawled with little or no oversight," she said in a phone interview this week. "They were doing general P.R., and often the events weren't even open to the public. A lot of it was community events where a member of Congress could call up and say send us a military band. What does that have to do with national defense?"

Her 2011 amendment failed. So did another she introduced the next year, when spending on bands had grown to $388 million.

Though the current $437 million price tag would barely qualify as a drop in the defense budget bucket of about $600 billion, it still dwarfs all other federal spending on music.

Leaders in the Pentagon quietly grumble that by focusing on bands, Congress is going after small potatoes. The military has for years proposed base closings that it estimates would save more than $2 billion

Master Sgt. Frank Carroll, a drummer who has been in the U.S. Army Blues for 25 years, packed up his gear after the military pageant. The military has about 6,500 musicians worldwide.

a year, but Congress has not acted on the politically troublesome proposals that could cut jobs in their districts.

The tension between the military's push for pomp and Washington's aversion to paying the piper is hardly a modern problem. At the outset of the Civil War, Union regiments enlisted lavish bands with as many as 50 musicians, sometimes complete with turbans and other exotic regalia. When forces converged in large encampments, one Union bandmaster later wrote, "the effect of the confusion of sounds produced can hardly be imagined."

By 1862, the Union had nearly 15,000 bandsmen, and the secretary of war issued an order limiting band size and pushing thousands of buglers, trombonists and other music makers out of the Army.

In 1927, Congress was considering an increase in pay and rank for military bandsmen. One senator opened hearings by noting that many military leaders "regard the band as a nuisance."

But the first witness, none other than John Philip Sousa, composer of the country's most famous marches, including the unofficial theme song of Independence Day, "The Stars and Stripes Forever," underscored music's power by saying that every great army since ancient times had relied on it.

"I do not believe that any nation that would go to war without a band would stand a chance of winning," he said. "You want something to put pep in a man, to make him fight."

These days, of course, troops ride into battle more often pepped up by a Bluetooth speaker on the dashboard, but the military still relies on bands for ceremonies and funerals.

Perhaps taking a cue from Congress, the military has started in recent years to cut back on its own. The Army has trimmed 600 band personnel since Congress started calling for reductions in 2011, and it plans to cut 270 more by 2019. The Marines and Navy cut two active-duty bands, and the Air Force cut three. A Pentagon spokesman said it was unclear whether decreasing the number of bands would decrease costs, since the cuts would mean more travel for the remaining musicians, but Pentagon figures show more than 90 percent of costs cover personnel.

Even with troop reductions, the military has no plans to curtail the main functions of its musicians, which range from playing on the White House lawn and at Arlington National Cemetery to playing in dusty and distant forward operating bases.

"Military bands are a critical part of operations," said Mark Wright, a Defense Department spokesman. "They inspire, they build a rapport with our citizens and foreign nations. The types of operations we do may be hard to understand, but everyone understands music."

Military Expects More Shopping Money, if Not All Trump Seeks

BY CHRISTOPHER DREW | MARCH 2, 2017

OVER THE NEXT two weeks, the military services will be scrambling to get their wish lists in front of top defense officials, hoping their requests for more troops, planes, ships and missiles will be stuffed into President Trump's proposed $54 billion increase in the Pentagon budget.

Never mind that Congress is unlikely to approve the full amount. Or that it is not clear if the Pentagon, which views Russia as the biggest threat, and the new president, who is mainly focused on defeating the Islamic State, agree on the priorities.

The services are betting that Mr. Trump will eventually win a large enough chunk of the money so that they can do a bit of everything, like reversing recent declines in the number of soldiers and Marines and breaking logjams over how many high-tech jets and ships they can afford to build.

But there are no guarantees, and the battle over next year's federal budget will be ferocious. Democrats have vowed to block the president's proposal to strip the $54 billion from domestic programs and shift it to the military. Nearly everyone expects the fight to drag on for months.

On Thursday, Mr. Trump helped set the stage, traveling to a shipyard in Newport News, Va., for an action-movie-like backdrop to tout his plans to build the armed forces. Speaking in the hangar bay of the nuclear-powered aircraft carrier Gerald R. Ford, which this year will become the nation's largest and most powerful floating fortress, Mr. Trump said the Navy — and other military services — must grow and modernize. The 100,000-ton vessel, the first of a new, more technologically advanced carrier class, cost about $13 billion after cost overruns and years of delay.

"We will make it easier for the Navy to plan for the future and thus to control costs and get the best deals for the taxpayer," the president said. "The same boat for less money, the same ship for less money, the same airplanes for less money."

Mr. Trump has complained about the cost estimates for new Air Force One planes to be built by Boeing, and he has pressed executives at Lockheed Martin to lower the cost of the F-35 Joint Strike Fighter. Whether that personal negotiating strategy can be applied across the breadth of the military's shopping is untested.

The president's aides have told the services to turn in their wish lists by March 16, and Defense Department and White House officials will plug in the final breakdown before submitting a budget to Congress, probably in May.

In a speech last September, Mr. Trump complained that President Barack Obama had cut the number of soldiers and Marines too sharply as the Pentagon shifted to special operations troops and armed drones to hunt terrorists. He also lamented that the Navy had fewer than half the ships it had under President Reagan.

He said then that the Army should hire 50,000 soldiers to get back to 540,000, and he supports a Navy plan to increase its fleet to 355 ships from 276. That plan calls for the Navy to buy more destroyers and start building three nuclear-powered attack submarines a year instead of two.

But Mr. Trump has also called for a more isolationist foreign policy and has said that American allies should pick up more of the bill for defending themselves. And even central tenets of military strategy are in question. At the same time Mr. Trump has been criticized by lawmakers from both parties for cozying up to Russia, his defense secretary, James Mattis, a retired Marine general, has described that country as America's "principal threat."

As a result, independent analysts said, it is hard to square the president's foreign and defense policies or know what his final priorities would be if Congress only approved part of the money he is seeking.

President Trump on Thursday in Newport News, Va., where the aircraft carrier Gerald R. Ford is being completed.

"It is not clear to me why we would need 355 ships if our foreign policy says we are going to reduce our commitments around the world and let allies do more for their own defense," said Todd Harrison, a military budget expert at the Center for Strategic and International Studies, a bipartisan Washington research group.

"And if you want to build a military more suited to deter Russia and China than to deter terrorists, it is a very different capability that you want to buy," Mr. Harrison said. "That is something that the Trump administration has not really rationalized yet."

Mr. Obama approved a series of sophisticated new weapons projects, including a new long-range bomber for the Air Force and massive ballistic missile submarines for the Navy. So the debate within the Pentagon now is not so much about pitting the services against one another to see whose pet project will survive as it is about determining how much money is needed to keep all the big projects going.

The Air Force, for instance, has been trying to expand production of the F-35 while also building new aerial-refueling tankers, modernizing nuclear missile systems and building the new stealth bombers.

Mr. Obama's last budget plan had forecast a $35 billion increase in Pentagon spending in the 2018 fiscal year to pay for all these programs. Mr. Trump's proposal, which would increase the defense budget to $603 billion, is $19 billion, or about 3 percent, higher than Mr. Obama's.

Other Republicans, such as Senator John McCain of Arizona, the chairman of the Senate Armed Services Committee, contend that even more is needed to maintain a technological edge over Russia and China. He recently released a report calling for a broader "high/low" mix in weapons capabilities and greater spending on research into space, cyber and artificial intelligence technologies.

But analysts say that the ultimate figure will be decided less by the Pentagon's support for particular programs than in overall budget negotiations between Congress and Mr. Trump, who is trying to change the kind of deals that have been struck since a deficit-reduction law required cuts in federal spending.

Under the law, the Budget Control Act of 2011, the cuts had to be divided evenly between defense and nondefense programs. Mr. Obama and Congress agreed several times after that on annual budgets that exceeded the caps and split the increases 50-50 between defense and domestic programs.

But Mr. Trump's proposal on Monday to increase military spending by $54 billion and cut nonmilitary programs by the same amount would shatter that truce. It also would require changes in the budget law, and that would give Senate Democrats, who want to protect domestic programs, leverage to force Mr. Trump to compromise. They could filibuster any bill attempting to change that 50-50 split, and the Republicans would have difficulty assembling the 60 votes needed to stop the filibuster.

Given those dynamics, political analysts say the president will have to accept a smaller increase in military spending and provide more money than he wants for domestic programs.

Gordon Adams, who oversaw military budgets in the Clinton White House, said that while Mr. Trump would not get as much as he was asking for, he might still be able to tilt the spending balance toward the military.

"In the end, I think the budget caps will be adjusted upward again," he said, "and we might get an uneven deal where the caps are higher for defense than for the domestic programs."

MICHAEL D. SHEAR contributed reporting from Newport News, Va.

The Pentagon Is Not a Sacred Cow

EDITORIAL | BY THE NEW YORK TIMES | DEC. 13, 2017

HEALTH CARE, SOCIAL SECURITY, Medicare and other social programs are all on the chopping block as the Republican-led Congress scrambles to make up for the revenue lost to its planned tax cuts. The Pentagon, however, remains a sacred cow, destined to receive yet more money.

The military budget is now $643 billion. The actual and potential threats from Russia, China, North Korea and Islamic extremists are all serious, but giving the Pentagon another huge increase defies common sense. The Pentagon already wastes about one in five of the taxpayer dollars it receives, according to a Pentagon-commissioned study. And the United States, which has plenty of other urgent needs, already spends more on its military than the next seven countries combined.

The opening bid for the 2018 defense budget came from President Trump, who in May proposed $677 billion. That was $54 billion above a budget cap set by Congress in 2011, after the 2008 financial crisis led to demands for fiscal restraint. Then last month, Congress upped his ante by passing a 2018 military authorization bill that would increase spending to around $700 billion, some $85 billion above the legal cap. Mr. Trump signed that bill into law on Tuesday.

For the moment, that increase is a fiction. Before it can occur, Congress must remove the 2011 caps and appropriate the money. That is the focus of the present budget battle on Capitol Hill. Republican leaders reportedly want to increase military spending by at least Mr. Trump's original figure of $54 billion and nonmilitary spending by $37 billion. Democratic leaders are insisting on equal increases for both categories.

What's not clear is that the Pentagon needs any increase until it can get a handle on waste, which a 2015 study estimated at $125 billion, about one-fifth of its budget.

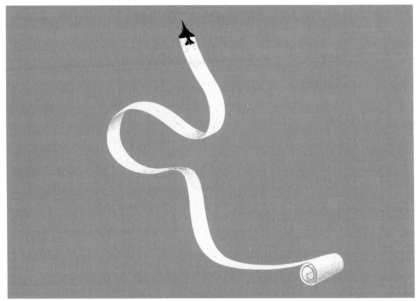

The Pentagon had a virtual blank check after the Sept. 11 attacks, as it went after Al Qaeda and the Taliban in Afghanistan and then turned its attention to overthrowing Saddam Hussein in Iraq. Military spending in 2017 is already as high as during the armed forces buildup of the 1980s. The proposed increase, coming after the United States has withdrawn thousands of troops from Iraq and Afghanistan, would take it even higher. Mr. Trump, bedazzled by men in uniform and enthralled by displays of weaponry, says more money is needed to build bigger and better forces. And senior commanders have lobbied hard for a big increase to upgrade a military they say lacks readiness, meaning the training and equipment needed to fight.

It's certainly true that the military, cut back after the Cold War, was strained during the 16 years of near constant war after Sept. 11. Yet the ground troops who are doing the actual fighting say there is no crisis, according to the analyst Mark Thompson of the Center for Defense Information at the Project on Government Oversight. Other experts say claims of a deteriorating military are exaggerated.

Some increases are understandable, even inevitable. For instance, from 2001 to 2012, the average cost per active service member grew by 61 percent, when adjusted for inflation, because of new and expanded benefits, increasing health care costs and pay raises. Those costs prompted the Pentagon to reduce personnel, says Todd Harrison, an expert with the Center for Strategic and International Studies.

But other increases arise from a dysfunctional congressional budget process complicated by lobbyists who woo lawmakers to back unneeded or extravagant weapons. That's how lawmakers wind up investing in programs that don't deliver, like the overbudget F-35 jet fighter, and modernizing the nuclear arsenal at an estimated cost of $1 trillion over the next 30 years, when smarter choices would cost less and still keep the country safe.

One encouraging sign is that the Pentagon's acquisition chief, Ellen Lord, is talking to Congress about moving away from high-tech toys that may no longer be relevant or affordable. Another is that the Pentagon has decided to launch its first (believe it or not) audit.

Like other federal agencies, the Pentagon can't have it all. The military is critical to national security. That does not give it license to be a poor steward of resources and gobble up tax dollars at the expense of other programs.

The Pentagon Doesn't Know Where Its Money Goes

EDITORIAL | BY THE NEW YORK TIMES | DEC. 1, 2018

The military finally submits to an audit, and the results are poor.

AFTER DECADES OF ducking the legal requirement that it undergo a thorough financial audit, the Pentagon finally opened up its books to 1,200 outside accountants and analysts. The report was recently completed, and here's the good news: The Army Corps of Engineers (most of it, anyway) and the Military Retirement Fund passed the audit.

The bad news: The Army, Navy, Air Force and Marines and most other divisions failed, which means they were unable to show that they were properly keeping track of their finances and assets.

The Pentagon has long prided itself on being a "can do" organization, firmly committed to protecting the nation. But when it comes to husbanding the billions of taxpayer dollars that pay for the vast military establishment, defense leaders have had less exacting standards.

"We failed the audit," Deputy Defense Secretary Patrick Shanahan told reporters with a curiously nonchalant air. "We never expected to pass it."

The Pentagon failed the audit largely because there are serious gaps in the financial controls that guide it, the world's largest military organization. It has $2.7 trillion in assets (weapons, bases and such) and $2.6 trillion in liabilities (mostly the costs of military personnel and retirees). Basically, the auditors couldn't account for where all the money went because of flaws in information technology systems.

That laxity — and the prospect of tax dollars flowing to boondoggles — would be concerning at any time. But it is especially worrisome when the federal budget deficit has skyrocketed to $779 billion — and the military is insisting it needs more money.

In a way, Mr. Shanahan's attitude is understandable. The Pentagon is an enormous bureaucracy — three million people, 15,700 aircraft, 280 ships, 585,000 facilities at 4,700 sites worldwide, an annual budget of $700 plus billion — and some experts say that expecting a clean bill of health on the first audit was never realistic.

Yet the Pentagon had nearly three decades to prepare for this accounting Judgment Day. While federal agencies were mandated by Congress in 1990 to begin performing annual financial audits, the Pentagon resisted for so long that it became the last one to comply with the law. Private companies, accountable to shareholders, couldn't get away with that.

But audits are hard work; most defense officials aren't business experts; and to some, bookkeeping and other management operations just aren't a priority in wartime, which since Sept. 11, 2001, has been a permanent state.

Most important, the Pentagon is skilled at bucking Congress, which is what it did all those years. This, even though the Government

Accountability Office, a government watchdog, put the Defense Department on its list of agencies vulnerable to fraud, waste and abuse in 2015.

The Pentagon was granted a virtual blank check to fight terrorism, and it still gets most of what it wants. It accounts for more than half of the federal discretionary spending, with a budget greater than the military spending of the next seven countries combined, including China and Russia.

So what did the audit — which cost some $413 million and covered every military asset, from buildings, fences, storage tanks, planes, computers, spare parts, invoices, purchase orders and contracts — find?

There are major flaws in how the Pentagon handles its information technology. The flaws include failing to revoke the credentials of former employees and using systems that can be hacked.

Officials said the auditors accounted for all major military equipment, even discovering $53 million worth of uninstalled missile motors at Hill Air Force Base in Utah that were cataloged erroneously as "not in working condition." That's an improvement from January, when defense officials acknowledged that they had lost track of 39 Black Hawk helicopters.

But the Pentagon was found to lack the systems and controls needed to "provide assurance over the existence, completeness and the valuation of inventory and related property recorded in the financial statements." In all, the audit identified 20 "material weaknesses" that "could adversely affect DoD's financial operations."

They discovered ineffective payment systems, outdated financial management information technology systems, and an inability to substantiate that Pentagon real estate assets were properly cataloged and valued, among other complaints.

The auditors estimated that the Pentagon made "improper payments" — which lacked sufficient or appropriate documentation or approvals — of $957 million in 2017 and $1.2 billion in 2018. While even that larger amount is a fraction of the overall Pentagon spending, such payments grew by 25 percent over those two years, a worrying trend that needs to be reversed.

Anyone expecting the discovery of pilfered funds will be disappointed. The audit wasn't looking for fraud — which generally refers to malicious illegal activities — and Defense Department officials said it found none. (Different audits examine different aspects of an organization.)

Its purpose was to determine whether accounts could be reconciled, making the results less sexy, perhaps, but still important. The inability to accurately track how money is spent makes it impossible to know whether precious resources are going to the right places, undermining the Pentagon's ability to be successful in its far-flung missions around the globe.

But it would be misleading to imply that such an immense bureaucracy is not also experiencing actual fraud, abuse or waste. Cost overruns and performance issues with such major weapons as the F-35 fighter jet and missile defense systems have been well documented in the past, raising doubts about the Pentagon's ability to responsibly manage taxpayer dollars.

And the Special Inspector General for Afghanistan Reconstruction has spent six years documenting more than $400 million in questionable costs, unfinished projects and poorly executed programs, and pursuing 132 criminal convictions, in Afghanistan, the site of America's longest-running war.

Last month, for example, a former recruiter of language interpreters for the American military was charged in an alleged scheme to recruit unqualified interpreters to work with American combat forces in Afghanistan. And in September, the former owner of a now defunct marble mining company in Afghanistan was found guilty in federal court for his role in defrauding the Overseas Private Investment Corporation and defaulting on a $15.8 million loan.

The unfavorable audit results come at an awkward time. A recent congressionally mandated study reached the alarming conclusion that despite all the money spent on defense, the United States today is so weakened that it "might struggle to win, or perhaps lose, a war against China or Russia." The study also found that America's military superiority and technological edge over those two major adversaries has eroded.

The Pentagon, defense hawks in Congress and defense contractors relentlessly push for bigger military budgets and will continue to do so. The commission that did the study recommended future annual increases of 3 percent to 5 percent above inflation, which could give the Pentagon a budget of $972 billion per year by 2024, a cumulative increase of 44 percent over the current budget, according to Taxpayers for Common Sense. But throwing more money at the Pentagon doesn't automatically make it more effective. Nor does it translate into better national security, as America's "forever wars" in Afghanistan and elsewhere demonstrate.

The nation needs to be more honest about the choices it is making (investing trillions more dollars in the nuclear arsenal is especially foolhardy) and realize that other investments — in diplomacy and development overseas, in job training and infrastructure projects at home — are also crucial to national security.

Defense Secretary Jim Mattis and his leadership team deserve credit for finally opening the books for an audit, thus providing a baseline against which the management of future spending can be measured.

Before rushing to push Pentagon spending even higher, however, Congress, which has shirked its vital oversight role, would be well advised to make sure that critical reforms are undertaken by a stubbornly change-resistant bureaucracy, so Americans can be certain their tax dollars are being spent effectively.

These Toilet Seat Lids Aren't Gold-Plated, but They Cost $14,000

OPINION | BY CHARLES GRASSLEY | DEC. 19, 2018

The Pentagon has to clean up its confusing and wasteful budget.

IN A JULY 21, 2017, MEMO, the secretary of defense, James Mattis, made promising comments about his ambitions to end wasteful spending at the Pentagon. He wrote that he expected "leaders at all levels in the department to exercise the utmost degree of stewardship over every penny" spent and that "only by instilling budget discipline, by establishing a culture of cost awareness, and by holding ourselves accountable, can we earn the trust and confidence of the Congress and the American people that we are the best possible stewards of taxpayer dollars."

I've spent more than three decades reviewing egregious spending at the Defense Department. The sentiments expressed in the memo were encouraging, so much so that I sent Secretary Mattis a letter of support. Since then, however, it seems the department has done very little to change its ways.

Over the past few months alone, the Defense Department has had to explain why it's been paying $14,000 for individual 3-D printed toilet seat lids and purchasing cups for $1,280 each. These are just the latest examples on a long list of unacceptable purchases made by the department, including $436 for hammers in the 1980s, and $117 soap dish covers and $999 pliers in the 1990s.

These wasteful expenditures reflect major underlying financial problems at the department, whose 2019 budget is more than $700 billion. If it had its financial house in order, overpriced parts and contracts might have been detected before ever being approved. Effective internal controls to catch and deter fraud, waste, abuse and theft serve as a firewall that would help prevent misuses of taxpayer dollars.

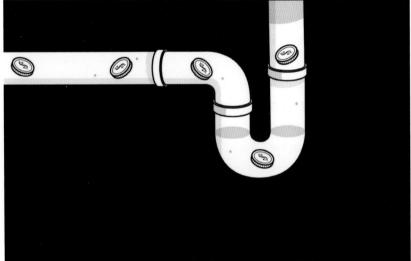

HARRY CAMPBELL

In 1990, Congress passed the Chief Financial Officers Act, which requires every federal agency to prepare a financial statement that is subject to audit by either the inspector general or an independent accounting firm. The auditors review the statements and render an opinion: clean, incomplete or failure. The goal is to hold government accountable by identifying and fixing financial problems. Since then, nearly all federal agencies have been able to produce a clean audit annually except for the Defense Department, because of its broken accounting systems.

The Pentagon is made up of many branches and agencies with multiple accounting systems. There are hundreds of different accounting systems with hundreds of different processes. This convoluted infrastructure is the perfect environment for waste, fraud and abuse. For example, with so many different systems in place it is easy — whether by design or accident — for supporting documentation like receipts and contract guidelines to vanish.

Without the ability to account for every dollar spent, there is no way for the Defense Department to produce a clean audit. There's also no way of knowing exactly how much or on what money is being spent. Taxpayers pay billions of dollars annually to fund Pentagon programs that are supposed to increase battle readiness, support military personnel and protect national security. Every wasted dollar weakens America's military might and takes resources away from our men and women in uniform and their families.

Last month, the Pentagon released the results of its recent full financial audit, produced at a cost of more than $400 million. They were disappointing but not surprising. Without an accounting system that can provide usable data, an audit is a waste of taxpayer money. What was surprising was the reaction from Pentagon officials. A deputy defense secretary told reporters, "We never thought we were going to pass an audit."

The tone of the comment speaks volumes about a lasting cavalier attitude at the Pentagon regarding reckless spending of taxpayer dollars. It would be smart of the department to fix its accounting systems before spending hundreds of millions of dollars on any future audit that will render the same predictable results.

Americans routinely balance their checkbooks, scrutinize their credit card statements and review their banking phone apps to manage their household budgets. There's no reason the Defense Department can't effectively do the same thing.

Some in Congress have tried to pressure the department to get its financial house in order. In 2015, I worked with a Democratic colleague, Joe Manchin of West Virginia, to try to pass the Audit the Pentagon Act, which would have provided incentives to the Defense Department to produce a clean audit. But the measure was not brought up for a vote. I also co-sponsored an amendment to the 2018 National Defense Authorization Act, the Pentagon's main spending bill, that would have required the Pentagon to report how much it spends preparing for audits and to verify data within its accounting systems. Again, the legislation went nowhere.

Ultimately Pentagon leaders must hold every department under them — including the Army, Navy, Air Force and Marine Corps — accountable for their financial failings. They need to heed the words of Secretary Mattis and live up to his promise that they'll be good stewards of taxpayer dollars.

CHARLES GRASSLEY is a Republican senator from Iowa and chairman of the Judiciary Committee.

CHAPTER 2

The Politics of Proliferation

Spending on the military has become so embedded in the United States economy that reducing it would have far-reaching consequences. The tangled incentives to produce jobs, keep businesses afloat and even to influence relationships with foreign governments means that building weapons and selling them is never straightforward. Simply trying to reduce the size of global weapons stockpiles is a game of balance, negotiation and public relations.

Arms Talks: A Signal and a Beginning

ANALYSIS | BY LESLIE H. GELB | JAN. 9, 1985

THE MEETING BETWEEN Secretary of State George P. Shultz and Foreign Minister Andrei A. Gromyko was in the end as much a foreign policy signal as it was a starting point for arms control.

As détente unfolded in the early 1970's, arms control negotiations led the way. As the two sides reach out toward each other this time, the thrust is more diffuse, and both are warier of arms limitations.

Diplomats on both sides intended the Geneva sessions as an unmistakable sign that after five years of saber-rattling and recriminations, the two superpowers are going to try to get along.

At the same time, Soviet and American officials remain skeptical about the prospects for arms control. And despite the progress made here and the agreement to continue talking, the two sides are still far apart.

PROCEDURAL AND PHILOSOPHICAL

Officials on both sides Tuesday night described the talks as procedural and philosophical, with few substantive exchanges on specific negotiating issues.

Moscow won a major procedural concession by getting the American side to agree to the objective of "preventing an arms race in space." Previously the Administration had been willing only to "discuss" the arms race in space.

But Mr. Shultz gained Soviet agreement that the negotiations on space include ground-based missile defense systems as well as space-based systems. Previously Moscow wanted to talk only about space-based missiles.

It had been agreed beforehand that offensive and defensive weapons would be part of future negotiations, so there was no change here.

On the agreement on having only one delegation to cover the three negotiating areas — space weapons, intercontinental-range nuclear forces and medium-range nuclear forces — Mr. Gromyko seemed to get the better of the bargain. Mr. Shultz had argued in favor of some greater separation of offense and defense, so that progress on offensive weapons would not be impeded by discussions of defense. But his associates said Tuesday night that the American side did not feel strongly about this point.

LESSENING TENSIONS

Cutting through the long hours of talks over the last two days and the formal language of the communiqué was this message: If the last five years was a period of rising tensions without direct confrontation, the coming period will be one of lessening tensions — even though significant arms control accords will be very difficult to conclude.

Before the gathering in this city of high-level meetings, Western and Eastern diplomats recognized that it would be far easier for Moscow and Washington to improve foreign policy atmospherics than to make the difficult concessions necessary to produce arms limitation pacts. All it would take to make better mood music would be to end the polemics and to sit down at the table with each other — as the two sides are doing now in Moscow to discuss trade and as they did in Geneva to talk about arms control.

But both Governments also understood, as interviews with officials on both sides made clear, that an improvement in overall relations required a resumption of the arms control dialogue. Soviet officials in Moscow have been telling visiting Westerners for several weeks that superpower relations are "one body," and that increasing trade cannot be separated from resuming arms control talks, which in turn cannot be separated from positive rhetoric. American officials, particularly in the State Department, make similar remarks.

THEORIES BUT NO CONSENSUS

Why, then, the push from both capitals for overall improvement? There are theories, but there is no consensus.

American hard-liners continue to think it is all a trick, a tactic to get the American people to lower their guard and reduce military spending. Hard-liners and moderates agree that Moscow does not want an all-out race with American technology in space-based defenses or in most other strategic areas. The costs to the Soviet economy of trying to match American technology are enormous.

Another theory favored by many specialists on Soviet affairs is that Soviet leaders know their economy is in trouble but refuse to make the necessary decisions to decentralize political control over it. Thus, the theory runs, they are looking for external help, much as they did in the early 1970's, in the form of trade, credits and Western technology.

Seeking external help is easier than making internal reforms. And so, many experts believe, Moscow wants to clear the way for more economic intercourse with the West, and to do that means resuming the arms talks that Soviet leaders broke off more than a year ago when the United States started deploying new medium-range missiles in Europe.

ADMINISTRATION'S VIEW

For the Reagan Administration's part, many officials came to believe that a bad relationship with Moscow was bad politics at home and meant bad relations with allies. As more and more officials in the Administration came to say, they had to show they were able to manage Soviet-American relations or else forfeit support from allies and the American public.

Passion for arms control within the Administration is still widely recognized to be modest. The division between the Pentagon hardliners and the State Department pragmatists is as deep as before, but advocates of making tough concessions to reach agreements are few, even in the State Department.

There is still a widespread view in the Administration that the Soviet Union is superior to the United States in strategic weapons. American officials are determined to demand larger concessions from Moscow than they are prepared to give. Moscow continues to maintain that there is a balance of forces and that concessions must be equal.

Thus, as Administration officials explained, their position here was to continue to demand that the first priority was for Moscow to reduce its arsenal of large and powerful land-based missiles.

NEW EMPHASIS ON DEFENSE

To make the equation even more complicated, President Reagan announced a year ago that he would give new emphasis to developing space-based defenses to protect people against missile attacks, and he argued that the whole basis of nuclear deterrence had to be reconsidered. Instead of relying on the power to destroy, he maintained, the emphasis should be on defense.

This idea, it seemed, both frightened the Russians and impelled them to return to the bargaining table. Soviet leaders demanded agreement to avoid the militarization of outer space.

The result was Geneva, a forum for the first time since the early 1970's for the two sides to discuss both offensive and defensive nuclear weapons. It had seemed for many years that the 1972 treaty sharply limiting ballistic missile defense systems had laid the defensive issue to rest. It had seemed for many years that negotiations on offensive weapons alone were difficult enough.

But the Geneva meeting put everything on the table once again, not so much because officials on either side believed there was much hope for arms limitation treaties, but because of the common realization that overall relations could not otherwise be improved.

Senator Blames Congress
for High Cost of Military

SPECIAL TO THE NEW YORK TIMES | JAN. 11, 1985

WASHINGTON, JAN. 10 — The chairman of a Senate subcommittee on military spending today denounced the increasingly popular idea of a freeze on the Pentagon budget and said Congress itself was largely to blame for the growing cost of the military.

In an interview, Senator Ted Stevens, Republican of Alaska and chairman of the Appropriations Subcommittee on Defense, said he might support cutting the $313.7 billion military budget proposed by President Reagan, but he warned that it would require Congress to give up some weapons systems cherished by lawmakers for the money they bring to constituents.

The Senate majority leader, Bob Dole, said Wednesday that Republican committee chairmen would probably agree to a freeze as the centerpiece of their package to reduce the budget deficit.

LEADERS AGAINST SPENDING FREEZE

But Mr. Stevens, along with Senator Barry Goldwater, Republican of Arizona, the chairman of the Armed Services Committee, has emerged as a champion of resistance to an across-the-board freeze of Federal spending that would include the military budget.

Both men have begun to build a case against a military freeze by threatening to cut programs that appeal to lawmakers' constituent interests.

On Monday, Mr. Goldwater said that if military cuts were necessary, he would support closing military bases, an idea he said would be "traumatic" to the members of Congress with bases in their home states.

Mr. Stevens said today that reductions in Mr. Reagan's military budget would require cuts in manpower and weapons systems popular in Congress.

As an example, Mr. Stevens pointed to the M-1 tank and the Navy's nuclear-powered attack submarines, both of which are programs Congress has built up faster than requested by the Pentagon. The M-1, made by Chrysler Corporation, is popular with lawmakers from Michigan, where it is manufactured, while the submarines were added at the urging of senators from the shipbuilding states of Connecticut and Virginia.

CUTS TRANSLATE TO JOBS

"Congress has made the defense bill a jobs bill," Mr. Stevens said. "We can cut, if they're willing to do the things you have to do. That means cutting manpower, and canceling orders for major nonstrategic weapons."

"Some of us are going to be looked at as unreconstructed hawks," he added, referring to himself and Mr. Goldwater. "But we're just trying to convey the impact."

A freeze in military spending, according to some estimates, would result in a 1986 military budget of $284.5 billion, about $29.2 billion less than the figure Mr. Reagan has approved.

But because military funds are budgeted to be spent over several years as bills for weapons come due, the immediate reduction in spending and the deficit would be much less. According to figures given to senators by the Office of Management and Budget, a freeze would only reduce the projected 1986 deficit by about $11.5 billion.

LINKS CUTS TO OTHER PROGRAMS

Mr. Stevens said he would support a military budget that amounted to a 3 percent increase on top of inflation. Mr. Reagan's proposal calls for a 6 percent increase after inflation. He said he would support this if other Government programs were frozen.

An aide to Mr. Stevens estimated that the Senator's proposal would cut about $8 billion from the military budget proposed by Mr. Reagan.

Because of the accumulated obligations of past military budgets, Mr. Stevens said, "That's about where we have to come out to get what other people are calling a freeze."

Mr. Stevens' subcommittee appropriates money within the limits set by the Budget and Armed Services committees.

In the interview, he lashed out at his colleagues, saying they "can't get it through their heads" that the military budget "is different" from other Federal programs because much of it consists of "bills coming due from the programs they insisted on passing last year."

Moreover, he said, because many weapons are bought on long-term contracts with penalty clauses for changes, "the cancellation charges for killing a weapon are almost equal to the cost of completing the order."

Linking Arms Cuts to Taxes

BY CLIFFORD KRAUSS | JAN. 7, 1992

WASHINGTON, JAN. 6 — Senator Phil Gramm, one of the most influential Republican lawmakers on budget policy, called today for a 5 percent cut in military spending by 1993 to allow the Government to raise the personal income tax exemption for every taxpayer by $416.

The conservative Texas Republican said his plan would result in a $466-a-year tax cut for a family of four whose income is $35,000. Because Mr. Gramm's proposal would cut military spending by more than the 1990 budget agreement provided for, it would bend, if not break, the agreement, which he helped to negotiate.

SIGNIFICANCE OF REMARKS

Mr. Gramm's proposed cut in military spending from $291 billion this year to $276.5 billion in the 1994 fiscal year and $275.3 billion by the 1995 fiscal year is thought to be close to the kind of cut President Bush is thinking of proposing in his State of the Union Message later this month. By making his proposal first, Mr. Gramm could protect Mr. Bush from criticism by Congressional conservatives who warn that military spending has already been sliced enough.

Mr. Gramm's comments are all the more significant because his state benefits substantially from military spending and has numerous military installations. Given the choice between sustaining the personnel size of the military or modernizing its equipment, Mr. Gramm said that he believed in a modern military that included a missile shield in space.

Mr. Gramm, speaking at a news conference, also suggested that any cuts in military spending beyond what he has proposed be equally divided between reducing the Federal deficit and increasing the personal income tax exemption. He said that there was "nothing magic" about his 5 percent proposal and that the final figure ought to be determined by the Defense Department.

"I believe that even in a world where the lion and lamb are about to lie down together, I want to be sure we're the lion," he said.

Mr. Gramm promoted his proposal as an alternative to several Democratic plans that would increase spending on social programs. One such plan, offered last week by Senator Jim Sasser, the Tennessee Democrat who is chairman of the Budget Committee, and Senator Paul S. Sarbanes, Democrat of Maryland, would increase Federal spending by $55 billion to stimulate the economy.

Satellite System for the Pentagon Brings Questions

BY TIM WEINER | JAN. 17, 1994

WASHINGTON, JAN. 16 — An elaborate satellite system created to help fight a long nuclear war with the Soviet Union is being prepared for launching next month, even as questions mount in Congress about its cost and need, given the diminished prospects for such a conflict.

Built to act as a space-based brain for nuclear war, the system would be a global switchboard — a network of satellites to relay military commands long after Washington and the Pentagon were destroyed in battle. It would also be one of the most expensive projects in the Pentagon's history.

Designed to allow all the military services to endure a six-month nuclear Armageddon, it has already survived efforts by the Air Force to eliminate it to save money.

PLANS ARE MODIFIED

The program, called Milstar for "military, strategic, tactical and relay system," was begun in the early 1980's as part of the Reagan Administration's $180 billion program to strengthen the nuclear arsenal. With the cold war over, the program is now being put forward in slightly scaled-back form and as a system that can be adapted for use in non-nuclear conflicts. But critics argue that this task could be handled by simpler equipment for less than half the cost.

"It's difficult to believe you could have a six-month nuclear war, but that's what our strategists planned," said Lou Rodrigues, a senior official of the General Accounting Office, the investigative arm of Congress.

"The Defense Department was committed to the program, and it's very difficult to get them to change gears," said Mr. Rodrigues, who has studied Milstar for three years. "The potential for an all-out nuclear war may be a thing of the past. But it's hard to make people break from the past."

COST ESTIMATE: $30 BILLION

While Milstar's ultimate cost remains unclear because of secrecy, technological uncertainty and its being seven years behind schedule, a variety of Government officials say it will approach $30 billion over the 20 years from the early 1980's to the turn of the century.

That is nearly as much as has been spent separately on the "Star Wars" missile defense system, which the Pentagon scaled back last year in favor of a more modest ground-based system. The Government has been criticized for taking up other expensive projects that were later abandoned, including the Superconducting Supercollider, which was canceled last year after $2 billion in spending.

The research and development costs of the satellite program remain secret, but an analysis of Pentagon records suggests that this part of the total expense has reached $8 billion.

In addition, the six Milstar spacecraft themselves are the most expensive communications satellites ever designed, costing up to $1.4 billion apiece. Combining the satellites with the rockets to put them in orbit, the space hardware part of the project will cost about $10 billion.

Billions more are being spent on thousands of portable computer terminals and data links to connect commanders, covert special operations units and generals in tractor-trailer trucks that would serve as mobile command centers.

SEEKING A SEAMLESS WEB

Milstar was conceived as the solution to decades of frustration over the problem of commanding American forces in wartime, said Pentagon officials and the Lockheed Missile and Space Company, the prime contractor for the project. It was to be an indestructible system coordinating missiles, bombers and submarines by creating a seamless web of leaders, weapons controls, communications and battlefield intelligence.

Once highly secret, the program was first exposed to general debate four years ago. In the first public Government report on the program, the Senate Armed Services Committee said, "the Department of Defense has not justified the extraordinary expense of this overdesigned system."

In the last two years, the system has been scaled down. Two satellites have been completed. The final four will be adapted to meet the needs of commanders fighting conflicts the size of the Persian Gulf war, and redesigned to make them less sophisticated and more practical, though no less costly.

To its supporters, Milstar is a revolutionary communications system that will make the tasks of 21st century battlefield commanders far easier.

"In order for commanders to maintain control in a rapidly moving battlefield environment, they need to be in contact," said Brig. Gen. Leonard F. Kwiatkowski, the Pentagon's program director for military satellite communications systems.

"An essential part of our ability to conduct warfare is rapidly deployable and survivable communications," he said. "Milstar's primary contribution to war fighting is that it is a protected, secure communications medium, with small rapidly mobile terminals designed to use the satellites and their global connectivity."

But to its critics, the program is a multibillion-dollar monument to the excesses of the cold war.

"I think we're still too close to it to look back and see how ludicrous it is," said Joe Cirincione, a senior associate at the Henry L. Stimson Center, a Washington research institution that specializes in foreign policy and military issues. "Milstar is a gross waste of money, and there are far cheaper ways to provide for that military mission."

A team of analysts from the Rand Corporation reported last month that despite the redesigning, the system may still be too expensive. Milstar remains "to a significant degree a system designed for a protracted nuclear war," said Dan Gonzales, a principal author of Rand's study.

General Kwiatkowski disagrees. "The most severe features or attributes associated with surviving nuclear war were taken off the satellite," he said. "While some features contribute to the system's ability to survive in any environment, including nuclear, to associate the communications features that are being provided by this system solely with nuclear war is a gross exaggeration."

Some of Milstar's more exotic secret electronics systems were canceled after the satellite was built because they were deemed too expensive or unnecessary. So one of the five-ton satellites will contain 878 pounds of ballast to compensate for the canceled systems.

The first Milstar launching is scheduled for Feb. 5 at Cape Canaveral, Fla. The House Government Operations Committee plans hearings on the satellites that week.

CANCELLATION STILL POSSIBLE

"I want to know if their enormous expense and questionable futuristic technology can be justified or are just a relic of the cold war we can no longer afford," said the committee's chairman, Representative John Conyers Jr., Democrat of Michigan.

The Pentagon could still cancel or alter the program and save billions of dollars, Mr. Rodrigues said. "The capability that we're seeking via the Milstar program could have been gotten, and still could be gotten, for about $18 billion less if they change their approach," he said.

Although many of Milstar's abilities remain secret, the original goals for the satellites included the ability to retreat from an orbit of 23,300 miles to a deep-space orbit of 110,000 miles to evade potential attackers. The goals also included the ability to foil enemy efforts to jam the satellites' messages and the ability to shield the spacecraft from the effects of nuclear explosions, including the electromagnetic pulse, a tidal wave of charged electrons that could devastate the nation's electronic circuits.

Despite Milstar's complexities, the first two satellites can handle only about 100 calls at a time, most of them very short "emergency action messages" like: "launch missiles." Because of anti-jamming methods, voice communications "sound like talking to Donald Duck," Mr. Rodrigues said.

Eric DeRitis, a Lockheed spokesman, said, "There is no satellite system that can do what's slated for this system." But Pentagon officials acknowledge that it will take years, and a large-scale war, before they know if Milstar can do what it was designed and redesigned to do.

Broad Ripples of Iraq War in Budgets of 2 Agencies

BY DAVID S. CLOUD AND JOEL BRINKLEY | FEB. 7, 2006

WASHINGTON, FEB. 6 — The costs of stabilizing and rebuilding Iraq will continue to ripple through the Pentagon and State Department budgets in 2007, under the proposal submitted to Congress on Monday.

The Pentagon, while seeking about $70 billion for additional war costs from now until Sept. 30, did not include the full cost of the war in its request for the fiscal year that begins Oct. 1. But in many ways, like seeking more of the combat vehicles that are heavily armored against improvised bombs and seeking money to attract new recruits and retain those already in uniform, the military's budget reflects continuing costs from the war.

The State Department is asking for continuing development support for Iraq, for a total of $479 million next year. While that is an eight-fold increase in the department's development aid, it is relatively little compared with the $20.9 billion that Congress has already approved for reconstruction. Much of that money, which was managed by the Pentagon rather than the State Department, has yet to be spent, or was diverted to security costs.

The State Department explained that the additional money for Iraq would be used to "sustain key Iraqi infrastructure." A senior department official said, "The money is for projects that are already up and running, not brand new programs." But given that many Iraqi reconstruction projects are incomplete or damaged because of sabotage, officials acknowledged that the definition was subjective.

A government audit last month found that millions of dollars in reconstruction aid to Iraq was lost, stolen or misspent.

The development financing for Iraq was the second highest proposed. Only Afghanistan would get more: $610 million. The administration said that money would used to pay salaries, build roads — essentially to pay for all manner of government services.

The money for Iraq and Afghanistan is part of a $33.65 billion State Department budget request, a 12 percent increase over the current year's budget.

With hidden bombs the leading cause of American casualties in Iraq, the Pentagon said it wanted $581 million to buy 3,000 more armored Humvees in the 2007 fiscal year's budget.

There are currently more than 26,000 Humvees in Iraq, of which more than 25,000 have some form of armor. But many of those have armor that was installed after the vehicles left the factory and is considered less effective. Army officials said they could not supply a separate breakdown on the number of factory-armored Humvees.

Over all, the Pentagon budget comes to $439.3 billion, a 7 percent increase over the $410.8 billion enacted by Congress last year. That request does not include the cost of operations in Iraq and Afghanistan, which has been financed in periodic stand-alone appropriations bills.

Tina Jonas, the Pentagon's top budget official, said the Pentagon budget included $1.9 billion in bonuses and incentives intended to retain senior enlisted personnel and warrant officers. Although re-enlistment numbers have been high, Pentagon officials are worried that they could lag, especially among midcareer enlisted personnel, as deployments in Iraq and Afghanistan continue.

The administration is requesting $5.1 billion, around $1 billion more than provided this year, to expand the number of special operations troops by around 4,000. Defense Secretary Donald H. Rumsfeld considers such forces vital for defeating terror groups and working with foreign militaries. By 2011, the Pentagon wants to increase the number of special operations troops by 14,000.

In foreign aid, the State Department is proposing a 13 percent drop in traditional foreign health, development and recovery aid, from an estimated $1.644 billion this year to $1.433 billion requested next year.

Some Eastern European and Central Asian states accounted for part of the drop. They will get sharply reduced aid, or none at all. The way the department put it, these states had "graduated" and did not need aid any longer. Bulgaria, Croatia and Romania would for the first time in recent years get no economic assistance next year.

But department officials noted that additional aid was delivered in many other ways, including democracy-promotion programs and H.I.V. and AIDS initiatives.

Foreign military assistance increased by just over 2 percent, to $4.84 billion, from $4.72 billion. While Romania, as an example, would get no economic aid, the administration proposes spending $1.6 million on military assistance there.

The weapons budget at the Pentagon provides both for the immediate needs of forces in combat and for costly long-term projects that have little bearing on the war.

The request allocates $1.6 billion on 132 unmanned aircraft, which Pentagon officials say are needed to provide better surveillance of suspected terror groups and other unconventional enemies. Last year, the Pentagon spent virtually the same amount and built 125 of this type of aircraft.

Among the bigger ticket items are requests for $3.7 billion for the Army Future Combat Systems, a combination of 18 digitally connected combat vehicles and other equipment. The program is expected to cost $22 billion by 2011.

Proposed Military Spending Is Highest Since WWII

BY THOM SHANKER | FEB. 4, 2008

WASHINGTON — As Congress and the public focus on more than $600 billion already approved in supplemental budgets to pay for the wars in Iraq and Afghanistan and for counterterrorism operations, the Bush administration has with little notice approached a landmark in military spending.

The Pentagon on Monday will unveil its proposed 2009 budget of $515.4 billion. If it is approved in full, annual military spending, when adjusted for inflation, will have reached its highest level since World War II.

That new Defense Department budget proposal, which is to pay for the standard operations of the Pentagon and the military but does not include supplemental spending on the war efforts or on nuclear weapons, is an increase in real terms of about 5 percent over this year.

Overall since coming to office, the administration has increased baseline military spending by 30 percent, a figure sure to be noted in coming budget battles as the American economy seems headed downward and government social spending is strained, especially by health-care costs.

Still, the nation's economy has grown faster than the level of military spending, and even the current colossal Pentagon budgets for regular operations and the war efforts consume a smaller portion of gross domestic product than in previous conflicts.

About 14 percent of the national economy was spent on the military during the Korean War, and about 9 percent during the war in Vietnam. By comparison, when the current base Pentagon budget, nuclear weapons and supplemental war costs are combined, they total just over 4 percent of the current economy, according to budget experts. The base Pentagon spending alone is about 3.4 percent of gross domestic product.

"The Bush administration's 2009 defense request follows the continuously ascending path of military outlays the president embraced at the beginning of his tenure," said Loren Thompson, a budget and procurement expert at the Lexington Institute, a policy research center. "However, the 2009 request may be the peak for defense spending."

Pentagon and military officials acknowledge the considerable commitment of money that will be required for continuing the missions in Iraq and Afghanistan, as well as efforts to increase the size of the Army, Marine Corps and Special Operations forces, to replace weapons worn out in the desert and to assure "quality of life" for those in uniform so they will remain in the military.

Yet those demands for money do not even include the price of refocusing the military's attention beyond the current wars to prepare for other challenges.

Senior Pentagon civilians and the top generals and admirals do not deny the challenge of sustaining military spending, and they acknowledge that Congress and the American people may turn inward after Iraq.

"I believe that we need to have a broad public discussion about what we should spend on defense," Adm. Mike Mullen, chairman of the Joint Chiefs of Staff, said Friday.

Defense Secretary Robert M. Gates and Admiral Mullen have said military spending should not drop below 4 percent of the national economy. "I really do believe this 4 percent floor is important," Admiral Mullen said. "It's really important, given the world we're living in, given the threats that we see out there, the risks that are, in fact, global, not just in the Middle East."

Geoff Morrell, the Pentagon press secretary, said Mr. Gates and the senior Pentagon leadership were well aware that the large emergency spending bills for the war, over and above the Pentagon base budget, would at some point come to an end.

"The secretary believes that whenever we transition away from war supplementals, the Congress should dedicate 4 percent of our G.D.P. to funding national security," Mr. Morrell said. "That is what he believes to be a reasonable price to stay free and protect our interests around the world."

No weapons programs are canceled in the new Pentagon budget, officials said; in fact, steadily increasing base defense budgets and the large war-fighting supplemental spending packages have made it easier for the Pentagon to avoid some tough calls on where to trim.

"But I think it's doubtful the nation will sustain this level of defense spending," said Steven Kosiak, vice president for budget studies at the Center for Strategic and Budgetary Assessments.

The 2009 military spending proposal will be the 11th year of continuous increases in the base military budget, he added.

War-fighting supplement spending measures are outside the base Pentagon budget, an issue that has angered some in Congress. Pentagon officials have proposed a $70 billion special war budget just to carry on operations from Oct. 1, the start of the fiscal year, into the early months of the next presidency.

Another supplemental spending proposal is expected before October, but after Gen. David H. Petraeus, the senior commander in Iraq, reports to Congress on his recommendations for troop levels through the end of 2008.

Any budget proposal is more than just a list of personnel costs and weapons to be purchased, as it lays out the building blocks of military strategy. Democrats vow to scrutinize the budget, the last by this president.

Senator Jack Reed of Rhode Island, who visited Iraq again last month, said that expanding the ground force as proposed in the new budget was an important step to relieve pressure on the Army and Marine Corps — one he would support even though he said it came too late.

Mr. Reed, a Democrat and a senior member of the Armed Services Committee, said demands of the counterinsurgency wars in Iraq and

Afghanistan raised questions on whether troops were receiving sufficient training, and were instead surrendering skills across a broader range of combat missions.

"It's going to require a rebalancing," he said. "It's going to require budget decisions that'll be very difficult."

U.S. Seeks $3 Billion for Pakistani Military

BY ERIC SCHMITT AND THOM SHANKER | APRIL 2, 2009

WASHINGTON — In a new effort to bolster Pakistan's fight against Al Qaeda and the Taliban, the Pentagon is proposing a plan to spend about $3 billion over the next five years to train and equip Pakistan's military.

The money would include up to $500 million in an annual emergency war budget that the Obama administration will submit to Congress next week, Pentagon officials said Thursday. The money would pay for helicopters, night-vision goggles and other equipment, and for counterinsurgency training for Pakistan's special operations forces and Frontier Corps paramilitary troops.

But some influential House Democrats who praised the idea of helping the Pakistani military said the new program, called the Pakistani Counterinsurgency Capability Fund, would circumvent the State Department's role in overseeing security assistance to international allies.

"This extends a pattern of militarizing foreign assistance," Representative Howard L. Berman, a California Democrat who leads the House Foreign Affairs Committee, said in a telephone interview.

The new approach, which requires Congressional approval, would give responsibility to the Pentagon and its Central Command for consulting with Pakistan's military and determining what equipment and training it most needed to fight an Islamist militancy that is gaining momentum in the country's unruly tribal areas. The fund would also be used to replace equipment the Pakistani Army and the Frontier Corps lost in combat.

"It is a specific fund designed, again, to help the Pakistani forces develop specific capabilities — counterinsurgency capabilities," Gen. David H. Petraeus, the leader of the Central Command, told the House Armed Services Committee on Thursday.

General Petraeus and other senior American officials declined to provide details of the program until the administration sent Congress its budget request.

Military supporters of the program said it offered a speedier alternative to the traditional military assistance process overseen by the State Department, which critics say is slow to respond to the needs of a rapidly shifting counterinsurgency campaign. The traditional military aid program provides Pakistan about $300 million a year, but does not focus solely on counterinsurgency goals.

The new military assistance program would complement legislation calling for $7.5 billion in civilian aid over five years proposed by Senators John Kerry of Massachusetts and Richard G. Lugar of Indiana, the top Democrat and Republican on the Foreign Relations Committee.

The United States has provided Pakistan with more than $12 billion in military and economic assistance since the Sept. 11, 2001, attacks, including about $1 billion a year to reimburse Pakistan for fielding 100,000 forces along its border with Afghanistan. American lawmakers have complained that much of that money has disappeared into Pakistani government coffers with scant accountability and little progress to show.

Adm. Mike Mullen, the chairman of the Joint Chiefs of Staff, acknowledged Thursday that the United States had not imposed sufficient accountability measures on the money.

"There hasn't been an audit trail, and there haven't been accountability measures put in place, and there needs to be for all the funds," Admiral Mullen said in an interview with the editorial board of The New York Times. "So we're going to do that. For this counterinsurgency money, which is important, it is critical that it goes for exactly that and nowhere else."

Admiral Mullen, who has worked extensively to build a relationship with the Pakistani army chief of staff, Gen. Ashfaq Parvez Kayani, noted that the Pakistani military had difficulties transforming from a military that recruited, trained, deployed and promoted its officers based on performance along the eastern front with India to one that focused instead on terrorists and insurgents within its own borders. "That's not going to change overnight," he said.

Insurgents and terrorists operating in Pakistani safe havens are plotting attacks against targets in both Afghanistan and Pakistan, the admiral said. "The Taliban, in particular, are going both ways now," he explained. "They are coming toward Islamabad and they are actually going toward Kabul. I'm completely convinced that the vast majority of the leaders in Pakistan understand the seriousness of the threat."

Admiral Mullen also cited the significance of the Congressional legislation to increase civilian aid to Pakistan, which President Obama has endorsed. The admiral said that aid would be seen as a positive sign of American long-term commitment to Pakistan.

ERIC SCHMITT reported from Washington, and **THOM SHANKER** from New York.

As Wars End, a Rush to Grab Dollars Spent on the Border

BY ERIC LIPTON | JUNE 6, 2013

TUCSON — The nation's largest military contractors, facing federal budget cuts and the withdrawals from two wars, are turning their sights to the Mexican border in the hopes of collecting some of the billions of dollars expected to be spent on tighter security if immigration legislation becomes law.

Half a dozen major military contractors, including Raytheon, Lockheed Martin and General Dynamics, are preparing for an unusual desert showdown here this summer, demonstrating their military-grade radar and long-range camera systems in an effort to secure a Homeland Security Department contract worth as much as $1 billion.

Northrop Grumman, meanwhile, is pitching to Homeland Security officials an automated tracking device — first built for the Pentagon to find roadside bombs in Afghanistan — that could be mounted on aerial drones to find illegal border crossers. And General Atomics, which manufactures the reconnaissance drones, wants to double the size of the fleet under a recently awarded contract worth up to $443 million.

The military-style buildup at the border zone, which started in the Tucson area late in the Bush administration, would become all but mandatory under the bill pending before the Senate. It requires that within six months of enactment, Homeland Security submit a plan to achieve "effective control" and "persistent surveillance" of the entire 1,969-mile land border with Mexico, something never before accomplished.

For military contractors, that could be a real boon. "There are only so many missile systems and Apache attack helicopters you can sell," said Dennis L. Hoffman, an Arizona State University economics

A Border Patrol agent near towers with radar, cameras for day and night, and a laser pointer, part of a system built by Boeing.

professor who has studied future potential markets for the defense industry. "This push toward border security fits very well with the need to create an ongoing stream of revenue."

Since 2005, the number of Border Patrol agents has doubled to 21,000, and the stretches protected by pedestrian or vehicle fencing have grown to 651 miles as of last year from 135. But there are still large swaths where people trying to enter the United States illegally have good odds of success, particularly in rural Texas. And with budget cutting in the past two years, money for surveillance equipment along the border has been pared back.

"The main gap in our ability to provide a more secure border at this point is technology," Mark S. Borkowski, the head of acquisitions for Homeland Security's Customs and Border Protection, told participants at a border security industry conference in March.

Military contractors have not played a significant role in lobbying for the passage of the immigration legislation, which includes $4.5 billion to bolster border security over the next five years.

But teams of lobbyists, including former Senator Alfonse M. D'Amato, a New York Republican, and Benjamin Abrams, a former top aide to Representative Steny H. Hoyer, a Maryland Democrat and House minority whip, have already been pressing Homeland Security officials and lawmakers on behalf of their clients, efforts that have been backed up with millions of dollars of industry campaign contributions.

Homeland Security would have to decide, in consultation with Congress, how to divide the money — on long-range cameras, radar systems, mobile surveillance equipment, aircraft or lower-tech solutions like more border agents or physical fences — decisions that would determine how various contractors might fare.

"It has been a tough time for the industry: people have been laid off or furloughed," said James P. Creaghan, a lobbyist who represents a small Texas company, Personal Defense, which is trying to sell more night-vision goggles to Homeland Security. "This could help out."

Northrop has won some important allies on Capitol Hill, including Senator Thomas R. Carper, Democrat of Delaware, the chairman of the Homeland Security and Governmental Affairs Committee, who is urging the department to invest more in Northrop's drone-mounted surveillance system, called Vader. General Atomics, which Mr. D'Amato represents, has so much support in Congress that it has pressed Homeland Security in recent years to buy more Predator drones than the department has the personnel to operate, so they often sit unused, according to an agency audit.

The specific requirement in the legislation now before the Senate is that Homeland Security must install surveillance equipment or other measures that would allow it to apprehend or turn back 9 out of 10 people trying to illegally enter across all sectors of the southern land border. The department would be prohibited from moving

The Joint Intelligence Operations Center in Tucson, which coordinates border enforcement, monitoring over 4,100 agents.

ahead with the "pathway to citizenship" for immigrants already in the United States until this new security strategy is "substantially operational."

The bill is scheduled to be taken up for debate on the Senate floor next week, and certain Republicans have already drafted amendments that would make the requirement even more demanding, explicitly mandating that the 90 percent standard be achieved before the pathway to citizenship can proceed.

The Tucson area, for years the busiest crossing point for illegal immigrants, has served as the testing ground for the federal government's high-technology border effort, although even senior Homeland Security officials acknowledge it got off to a poor start.

Boeing was selected back in 2006, when the last major push by Congress to rewrite the nation's immigration laws was under way, to create a "virtual fence" that would use radar and video systems to identify and track incursions, information that would then be beamed to regional command centers and border agents in the field.

But the ground radar system at first kept shutting down because of faulty circuit breakers, audits found, while the towers installed for the mounting of radar and advanced long-range cameras swayed too much in the desert winds. Even rainstorms snarled things, creating countless false alerts.

"It should have been pretty simple," Mr. Borkowski said in a recent speech of the troubled $850 million project. "We weren't frankly smart enough."

Critics say the government often is too fixated on high-technology solutions. C. Stewart Verdery Jr., a former Homeland Security official who now runs a lobbying firm, said federal officials should instead focus their limited resources on making it harder for illegal immigrants to work in the United States, an approach that would serve as an effective deterrent.

"Where are you going to get the biggest bang for the buck?" Mr. Verdery said. "Enforcement of the workplace is probably the best area to invest more dollars."

But the technological solutions still have many advocates in Arizona, where Border Patrol officials contend that the equipment Boeing installed, despite its flaws, has fundamentally changed the cat-and-mouse game that plays out every day.

One recent afternoon, as the temperature in the Arizona desert hovered near 100 degrees, Border Patrol agents stationed inside a command center in Tucson were notified that a ground sensor had gone off. The command center, built under the Boeing contract, resembles the set from the Hollywood movie "Minority Report," with Border Patrol agents sitting in front of banks of computer terminals and oversize screens that allow them to virtually fly over huge expanses of open desert 70 miles away.

Using his computer, one agent pointed the long-range, heat-seeking camera at the location where the sensor had gone off. Within seconds,

A tower with cameras and radar to track illegal crossings.

black-and-white images of a group of men and women walking rapidly through the desert heat appeared on his screen. "One, two, three, four, five," the agent called out, counting until he reached 15 people in the group. He also carefully scanned the images to see if any of the people were carrying large sacks, a sign of a possible drug delivery, or had any rifles or other weapons.

The Border Patrol radios lit up as he directed nearby agents on the ground to respond and called for backup from one of Customs and Border Protection's helicopters based in Tucson.

"What you see today is like night and day compared to what we had," said Cmdr. Jeffrey Self of the Border Patrol, who oversees the Tucson region. The Boeing system, along with the surge in Border Patrol agents, has resulted in a major drop in attempted illegal crossings, he said, with apprehensions dropping 80 percent since their peak in 2000, considered a sign of a drop in overall traffic.

But the system's weaknesses are still apparent. The computer terminal crashed while the search was under way, cutting off one agent's video feed. And on that recent afternoon, no air support was immediately available. The one helicopter nearby that was on duty was running low on fuel, so it did not arrive on the scene until 90 minutes later. Meanwhile, the Border Patrol agents at the Tucson command center lost the border crossers as they dropped into a ditch, taking them out of the line of sight of the camera and radar.

Apparently seeing Border Patrol trucks and the helicopter, the group realized it had been spotted and retreated back south, an agency spokesman said. The 15 were marked down as "turn backs."

Homeland Security has been preparing for more than a year to expand this system, under a new contract that would rely on proven surveillance technology. That is why the military contractors vying for the job will be asked in coming weeks to demonstrate their gear. The department also wants to identify a mix of equipment — some on fixed towers, others on trucks for mobility — so that officials can tailor uses to the different needs along the border.

Department officials said their choices would be driven by a determination of what the best available tools were for securing the border, not what the defense contractors or their lobbyists were pitching. Customs and Border Protection officials, said Michael J. Friel, a department spokesman in a statement, are "dedicated to continuing this progress towards a safer, stronger and more secure border."

Arms Sales to Saudis Leave American Fingerprints on Yemen's Carnage

BY DECLAN WALSH AND ERIC SCHMITT | DEC. 25, 2018

CAIRO — When a Saudi F-15 warplane takes off from King Khalid air base in southern Saudi Arabia for a bombing run over Yemen, it is not just the plane and the bombs that are American.

American mechanics service the jet and carry out repairs on the ground. American technicians upgrade the targeting software and other classified technology, which Saudis are not allowed to touch. The pilot has likely been trained by the United States Air Force.

And at a flight operations room in the capital, Riyadh, Saudi commanders sit near American military officials who provide intelligence and tactical advice, mainly aimed at stopping the Saudis from killing Yemeni civilians.

American fingerprints are all over the air war in Yemen, where errant strikes by the Saudi-led coalition have killed more than 4,600 civilians, according to a monitoring group. In Washington, that toll has stoked impassioned debate about the pitfalls of America's alliance with Saudi Arabia under Crown Prince Mohammed bin Salman, who relies on American support to keep his warplanes in the air.

Saudi Arabia entered the war in 2015, allying with the United Arab Emirates and a smattering of Yemeni factions with the goal of ousting the Iran-allied Houthi rebels from northern Yemen. Three years on, they have made little progress. At least 60,000 Yemenis have died in the war, and the country stands on the brink of a calamitous famine.

For American officials, the stalled war has become a strategic and moral quagmire. It has upended the assumptions behind the decades-old policy of selling powerful weapons to a wealthy ally that, until recently, rarely used them. It has raised questions about complicity in possible war crimes. And the civilian toll has posed a troubling dilemma: how to support Saudi allies while keeping the war's excesses at arm's length.

In interviews, 10 current and former United States officials portrayed a troubled and fractious American response to regular reports of civilians killed in coalition airstrikes.

The Pentagon and State Department have denied knowing whether American bombs were used in the war's most notorious airstrikes, which have struck weddings, mosques and funerals. However, a former senior State Department official said that the United States had access to records of every airstrike over Yemen since the early days of the war, including the warplane and munitions used.

At the same time, American efforts to advise the Saudis on how to protect civilians often came to naught. The Saudis whitewashed an American-sponsored initiative to investigate errant airstrikes and often ignored a voluminous no-strike list.

"In the end, we concluded that they were just not willing to listen," said Tom Malinowski, a former assistant secretary of state and an incoming member of Congress from New Jersey. "They were given specific coordinates of targets that should not be struck and they continued to strike them. That struck me as a willful disregard of advice they were getting."

Yet American military support for the airstrikes continued.

While American officials often protested civilian deaths in public, two presidents ultimately stood by the Saudis. President Obama gave the war his qualified approval to assuage Saudi anger over his Iran nuclear deal. President Trump embraced Prince Mohammed and bragged of multibillion-dollar arms deals with the Saudis.

As bombs fell on Yemen, the United States continued to train the Royal Saudi Air Force. In 2017, the United States military announced a $750 million program focused on how to carry out airstrikes, including avoiding civilian casualties. The same year, Congress authorized the sale of more than $510 million in precision-guided munitions to Saudi Arabia, which had been suspended by the Obama administration in protest of civilian casualties.

Nearly 100 American military personnel are advising or assisting the coalition war effort, although fewer than 35 are based in Saudi Arabia.

American support for the war met stiff headwinds this fall, when congressional fury over the murder of the Saudi dissident Jamal Khashoggi combined with worries over civilian deaths in Yemen.

In response, the Trump administration ended American air-to-air refueling of coalition warplanes over Yemen in November but has otherwise continued to support the war. This month, the Senate voted to end American military assistance to the war altogether, a sharp rebuke to the Trump administration, but the bill died when the House refused to consider it.

The civilian toll is still rising. According to the Armed Conflict Location and Event Data Project, November was the most violent month in Yemen since the group began tracking casualties in January 2016. There were 3,058 war-related fatalities in November, it said, including 80 civilians killed in airstrikes.

'EXPENSIVE PAPERWEIGHTS'

For decades, the United States sold tens of billions of dollars in arms to Saudi Arabia on an unspoken premise: that they would rarely be used.

The Saudis amassed the world's third-largest fleet of F-15 jets, after the United States and Israel, but their pilots almost never saw action. They shot down two Iranian jets over the Persian Gulf in 1984, two Iraqi warplanes during the 1991 gulf war and they conducted a handful of bombing raids along the border with Yemen in 2009.

The United States had similar expectations for its arms sales to other Persian Gulf countries.

"There was a belief that these countries wouldn't end up using this equipment, and we were just selling them expensive paperweights," said Andrew Miller, a former State Department official now with the Project on Middle East Democracy.

Then came Prince Mohammed bin Salman.

When the prince, then the Saudi defense minister, sent fighter jets to Yemen in March 2015, Pentagon officials were flustered to receive just 48 hours notice of the first strikes against Houthi rebels, two former senior American officials said. American officials were persuaded by Saudi assurances the campaign would be over in weeks.

But as the weeks turned to years, and the prospect of victory receded, the Americans found themselves backing a military campaign that was exacting a steep civilian toll, largely as a result of Saudi and Emirati airstrikes.

American military officials posted to the coalition war room in Riyadh noticed that inexperienced Saudi pilots flew at high altitudes to avoid enemy fire, military officials said. The tactic reduced the risk to the pilots but transferred it to civilians, who were exposed to less accurate bombings.

Coalition planners misidentified targets and their pilots struck them at the wrong time — destroying a vehicle as it passed through a crowded bazaar, for instance, instead of waiting until it reached an open road. The coalition routinely ignored a no-strike list — drawn up by the United States Central Command and the United Nations — of hospitals, schools and other places where civilians gathered.

At times, coalition officers subverted their own chain of command. In one instance, a devastating strike that killed 155 people in a funeral hall was ordered by a junior officer who countermanded an order from a more senior officer, a State Department official said.

The Americans offered help. The State Department financed an investigative body to review errant airstrikes and propose corrective action. Pentagon lawyers trained Saudi officers in the laws of war. Military officers suggested putting gun cameras on Saudi and Emiratis warplanes to see how strikes were being conducted. The coalition balked.

In June 2017, American officials extracted new promises of safeguards, including stricter rules of engagement and an expansion of the no-strike list to about 33,000 targets — provisions that allowed the secretary of state, then Rex W. Tillerson, to win support in Congress for the sale of more than $510 million in precision-guided munitions to the kingdom.

But those measures seemed to make little difference. Just over a year later, in August 2018, a coalition airstrike killed at least 40 boys on a packed school bus in northern Yemen.

Still, American leaders insisted they need to keep helping the Saudi coalition.

America's role in the war was "absolutely essential" to safeguard civilians, the general in charge of Central Command, Gen. Joseph L. Votel, told a charged Senate hearing in March.

"I think this does give us the best opportunity to address these concerns," he said.

WHAT THE U.S. KNOWS

In March, Prince Mohammed paid a visit to Washington, where he was feted by President Trump. As the two leaders sat in the White House, Mr. Trump held aloft a chart with price-tagged photos of warplanes and other weapons.

"$3 billion," Mr. Trump said, pointing to the chart. "$533 million. $525 million. That's peanuts for you."

The prince chuckled.

But in Congress, the mood was souring. In the March hearing, senators accused the Pentagon of being complicit in the coalition's errant bombing, and pressed its leaders on how directly the United States was linked to atrocities.

General Votel said the military knew little about that. The United States did not track whether the coalition jets that it refueled carried out the airstrikes that killed civilians, he said, and did not know when they used American-made bombs. At a briefing in Cairo in August, a senior United States official echoed that assessment.

"I would assume the Saudis have an inventory system that traces that information," said the official, who spoke anonymously to discuss

President Trump, meeting with Crown Prince Mohammed bin Salman of Saudi Arabia in March, bragged of American arms sales to the kingdom.

diplomatically sensitive relations. "But that's not information that is available to the U.S."

But Larry Lewis, a State Department adviser on civilian harm who worked with the Saudi-led coalition from 2015 to 2017, said that information was readily available from an early stage.

At the coalition headquarters in Riyadh, he said, American liaison officers had access to a database that detailed every airstrike: warplane, target, munitions used and a brief description of the attack. American officials frequently emailed him copies of a spreadsheet for his own work, he said.

The data could easily be used to pinpoint the role of American warplanes and bombs in any single strike, he said. "If the question was "Hey, was that a U.S. munition they used?" You would know that it was," he said.

Capt. Bill Urban, a spokesman for Central Command, did not deny the existence of the database, but said that American officers only used coalition data to carry out their core mission: advising on civilian casualties, sharing intelligence on Houthi threats and coordinating the midair refueling that ended in November.

"I will not speculate on how the United States could have used or compiled the information the Saudi-led coalition shared for some other function," he said in a statement. "That is not the mission these advisers were invited to Riyadh to perform. That is not the way partnerships work."

Other officials have said that collating information about use of American munitions in Yemen would be onerous and, ultimately, pointless. "What difference would it make?" the senior United States official in Cairo said.

But legal experts say such information could be significant. Inside the State Department, there have been longstanding worries about potential legal liability for the American role in the war. In August, the United Nations' human rights body determined that some coalition airstrikes were likely war crimes.

Under American law, customers of American weapons must follow the laws of armed conflict or future sales may be blocked, said Ryan Goodman, a former Defense Department attorney who teaches law at New York University.

Mr. Lewis, who left the State Department in 2017, said that in his experience, individual Saudi officers were often concerned or distressed by airstrikes that killed civilians but there was little institutional effort to reform the system.

The Joint Incidents Assessment Team, the body set up to investigate errant strikes, worked diligently at first, he said. But when its findings were made public, the Saudi Ministry of Foreign Affairs had removed any references that were critical of coalition actions.

Asked if that was the case, the Saudi ambassador to Yemen, Mohamed Al Jaber, said, "The JIAT is an independent team," and he referred any questions to them.

Obfuscation and impunity continue to characterize the coalition's airstrike campaign. The coalition rarely identifies which country carries out an airstrike, although the vast majority are Saudi and Emirati, officials say. In July, King Salman of Saudi Arabia issued an order lifting "all military and disciplinary penalties" for Saudi troops fighting in Yemen, an apparent amnesty for possible war crimes.

Over the summer, as Emirati warplanes pounded the Red Sea port of Hudaydah, General Votel and the defense secretary at the time, Jim Mattis, held at least 10 phone calls or video conferences with Saudi and Emirati leaders, urging them to show restraint, a senior American military official and a senior Western official said.

At least one of the conferences involved Mohammed bin Zayed, the crown prince of Abu Dhabi and the effective leader of the United Arab Emirates.

"The Saudis are decent partners," Gen. C.Q. Brown Jr., a former top commander of American air forces in the Middle East, said in an interview. "And sometimes our partners don't always do things we would expect."

Short of halting all weapons sales, critics say the United States could pressure the Saudis by curtailing its assistance to the air war. Hundreds of American aviation mechanics and other specialists, working under Defense Department contracts, keep the Saudi F-15 fleet in the air. In 2017, Boeing signed a $480 million contract for service repairs to the fleet.

But after the departure of Mr. Mattis, who resigned last week, the Defense Department will be helmed by Patrick M. Shanahan, an arms industry insider. Mr. Shanahan, the acting defense secretary as of Jan 1., spent more than three decades at Boeing, the F-15 manufacturer which has earned further billions from lucrative service contracts in Saudi Arabia.

Pentagon officials said that in his current job as deputy defense secretary, Mr. Shanahan had recused himself from decisions involving Boeing.

Daniel L. Byman, a professor at Georgetown University's School of Foreign Service, said that a more robust policy toward Saudi airstrikes would not just be good for Yemeni civilians — it would also help the Saudis.

"This war has been a strategic disaster for the Saudis," he said. The airstrikes have shown no sign of defeating the Houthis, and the Houthis' foreign ally, Iran, has gained from Saudi Arabia's clumsy prosecution of the war.

"The United States needs to use its power to promote peace and stability in Yemen," Mr. Byman said. "And it needs to protect its allies from themselves."

DECLAN WALSH reported from Cairo, and **ERIC SCHMITT** from Washington.

CHAPTER 3

Private Industry

Planes, submarines, tanks, helicopters: Someone designs,
tests and manufactures them. Military suppliers are some
of the largest, most profitable engineering companies in the
world, and their success is closely tied to the volatility of international politics. Their success and failure can, in turn, affect
global economic markets. But there are other, more shadowy
"services" sectors in modern warfare consisting of private
"security" firms that operate as small mercenary armies.
Private industry and the U.S. federal government are close
partners in weapons development, deployment and sales.

Defense Stocks Go on Offensive

BY ROBERT METZ | JAN. 8, 1980

SHARES OF LEADING defense issues soared again yesterday as investors
took an increasingly negative view of the chances for peace in the
Middle East.

There were delayed openings for shares of such disparate companies as Northrup and General Dynamics, both primarily military
suppliers, and Boeing, which is almost 90 percent dependent on the
commercial aircraft market.

To some observers, Boeing's rise was symptomatic of a frenzied
market in which any company with an aerospace orientation benefited, even without major military orders. Boeing was up 4 ⅞ on Friday
at 55 ⅛, a high for the stock and a breakout from an 18-month consol-
idation period in which prices ranged from about 40 to 52. Yesterday,
Boeing reached 58 ¾ and closed at 57 ⅛.

The first aerospace shares to open yesterday were those of such conglomerates as Rockwell International, Martin Marietta and TRW. Rockwell, for example, was up 2 ¾ on top of a 2-point gain to 49 ¼ on Friday. The military factor at Rockwell amounted to 36 percent of sales in the fiscal year ended September 1979. Military business accounted for a lesser percentage of earnings.

On Friday, Martin Marietta was up 3 ½ to 49, and the stock was strong again yesterday, reaching 51 ⅛ and closing at 49 ⅜. In 1978, Martin's aerospace sales were 42 percent of its total, and military earnings accounted for 21 percent.

Apparently, Rockwell was favored yesterday because it is an important factor in the space shuttle, which is regarded as essential for the military satellite program of the 1980's. Martin shares gained, it seems, because the company is the designated prime contractor for a new generation of intercontinental ballistic missiles as well as a leading supplier of advanced tactical weapons.

Northrop and General Dynamics opened around 11:30 A.M. yesterday. Northrop, up 6 ¾ points at the high yesterday, closed at 47 ⅞, after having closed on Friday at 45, up 5. The major reason for Northrop's strength was that President Carter, in an about-face, is now encouraging the development of a new fighter plane aimed purely at the export market. Northrop's F-5E, in a new version to be called the F-5G, is thought to be a leading contender for what could be a multibillion-dollar market.

General Dynamics, with a near-monopoly on nuclear submarines, was up 6 to 68 on Friday and touched 70 ¼ yesterday, closing at 68 ¾.

TRW was up 1 ⅛ to 40 on Friday and closed at 42 ½ yesterday. Action in these shares seemed to be in sympathy with the broader aerospace-defense move since the company is not a prime contractor for major military systems.

Wolfgang H. Demisch, aerospace analyst for Smith Barney, Harris Upham & Company, told the firm's salesmen in an all-office hook-up early yesterday that, for the very near term, the military stocks were "probably" reaching a peak, unless the Afghan insurgents were "unexpectedly successful."

However, he added, it was clearly a Wall Street disappointment that the Iranians had refused the good offices of United Nations Secretary General Kurt Waldheim to reach a face-saving solution to the hostage crisis even while Soviety military intervention was in progress near the Iranian border.

He also told the sales force that, because of growing fragmentation within the Western and third worlds, and purposeful Soviet expansionism, the 1980's would appear likely to be an environment of much greater international stress and tension.

"As near as I can tell, the Russians face massive economic and social problems with low productivity, a deteriorating birth rate and rising nationalistic pressures within the bloc," he said. "The Russians might be tempted to solve their problems by a more militant foreign policy."

In mid-December, aerospace analysts for Drexel Burnham Lambert Inc. said it was rather late to participate in the gains in military shares, that the "easy money" had already been made. They added, though, that the group with the strongest exposure to military spending might very well continue to outperform the market averages in the next six to 12 months.

They said yesterday that they continued to recommend aerospace companies, particularly Raytheon, Fairchild Industries and Northrop.

Eliot Fried Jr., who follows aerospace shares for Shearson Loeb Rhoades Inc., said that the outlook for the aerospace industry was good even before the Middle East crisis.

The inflation-adjusted increase of 5 percent a year in the military budget that the Carter Administration is now asking to maintain military parity with the Soviet Union would, in Mr. Fried's opinion, extend the aerospace cycle beyond the usual seven-year term.

"This defense cycle could last 10 and possibly 12 years," he said. He asserts that the multiples of such stocks as General Dynamics (7 to 8) and McDonnell Douglas (7.5) on 1980 earnings are "almost in line with the market as a whole."

Despite all this bullish sentiment, the shares of most military suppliers have more than doubled in the last year, causing some in Wall Street to feel that the possibility of further near-term gains is limited.

What is more, such companies as Boeing, McDonnell Douglas and Lockheed, which have large commercial aircraft components, could find some orders vulnerable because of a poor outlook for domestic airline profits in 1980.

Arms Makers Are the Top Beneficiaries; A Banner Budget for Arms Makers

BY EDWIN MCDOWELL | JAN. 20, 1980

LOVE IT OR LOATHE IT, the military-industrial complex is back in business. The tensions in Iran and Afghanistan have given the defense industry a multibillion dollar shot in the arm, and the economic consequences could mean more jobs, higher inflation, a larger Federal budget deficit, a strong stock market and an end to recessionary expectations.

The defense budget, after a steady decline in real terms every year from 1968 through 1976, will begin rising significantly when President Carter unveils his fiscal 1981 budget later this month. And it is likely to keep rising at least through the mid-1980's regardless of who is elected President.

"I certainly don't see anything on the world scene that would encourage me to think defense budgets will be lowered," said Laurence J. Adams, president of the Martin Marietta Aerospace Company. "Quite the opposite." Consider these developments:

• With SALT II now on the diplomatic back burner, defense officials expect additional spending for space technology, particularly as the Administration seeks to develop an array of defensive "smart weapons" capable of knocking down enemy ballistic missiles in space.

• By recently withdrawing its opposition to overseas sales of American warplanes, the Administration has freed United States manufacturers to compete for billions of dollars of orders that have been off-limits for the last two years. In addition, the State Department recently approved $280 million in sales of defensive military weapons to Taiwan, after a one-year suspension.

• A 100,000-man rapid deployment force to be whisked quickly to world trouble spots is planned and will entail the expenditure of billions of dollars for weapons, munitions and transport planes.

• The White House is talking about providing Pakistan with artillery, armor and antitank weapons. It is putting pressure on Japan to assume a bigger defense role. And defense industry officials say Japan could do so only by purchasing American military equipment. Defense officials also speculate that, denials notwithstanding, Washington may also eventually sell defensive weapons to China.

Investors have been quick to read the industrial impact of all these diplomatic maneuvers and as a result, the defense stocks are among the hottest on Wall Street.

"I would guess that since the start of the year, stocks of the major defense contractors have gone up 15 to 20 percent, on top of a similar amount during the last few weeks of 1979 after the Embassy seizure in Iran," said Wolfgang H. Demisch, aerospace industry analyst at Smith Barney Harris Upham & Company. "The investment community is aware that the world is becoming a nastier place and that it's likely to be more fragmented and hostile in the 1980's. That combination makes a helpful environment for military contractors."

Said William Perreault, a spokesman for the Lockheed Corporation: "Our stock moved from the $25 range to the $40 range over the last 60 days, but we were really surprised when our bonds also moved up substantially. We have $125 million in 4 ½ percent convertibles, and from a low of 61 in the past month they went up over 70."

Even before Soviet troops landed in Afghanistan, President Carter promised to increase the fiscal 1981 defense budget about $19 billion over 1980, to $157.5 billion, with real increases averaging 4.5 percent through fiscal 1985. Adjusted for an inflation rate of 9.3 percent, defense spending might well hit $200 billion in fiscal 1984.

But industry officials believe that events of the last few weeks will push defense spending even higher — not to the approximately 10 percent of gross national product devoted to defense during the Korean and Vietnam years, but high enough to develop the array of weaponry and manpower considered necessary to blunt any new Soviet adventurism. Despite the higher price tag on the new five year defense plan, President Carter said that the percentage of American G.N.P. devoted to defense "will remain steady at about 5 percent."

Only 26 percent of the current defense dollar is spent on weapons and hardware, with the remainder fragmented into many other categories. Of the $137.4 billion enacted for defense spending in fiscal 1980, according to the Pentagon, 29.3 percent is for military personnel (including military pensions), 30 percent for operations and maintenance (more than one-third of that for civilian employee payrolls), 10 percent for research and development, about 2 percent each for military construction and defense-wide contingencies, and 1 percent for family housing.

That means $35.8 billion for nuts and bolts procurement, although defense industry insiders say that the lion's share of defense budget increases will probably go for weapons and hardware.

The defense industry is considerably changed since the Vietnam era, particularly the aerospace sector, which has embarked on a steady diversification. "In calendar 1980, for the first time since before World War II, the aerospace industry's commercial sales will surpass defense sales — something like $20.2 billion civilian compared with $17.4 billion military," said Julian R. Levine of the Aerospace Industries Association of America. The Boeing Corporation, McDonnell Douglas, and Lockheed all have large orders for civilian airplanes, Mr. Levine said. They and the smaller American airplane manufacturers are likely to benefit from sales to foreign governments, some of which plan to overhaul their antiquated fleets in the next few years.

Some analysts profess astonishment at the recent run-up in Boeing stock, since defense constitutes only about 25 percent of Boeing's overall business ($8 billion in 1979) — a lot of dollars but not a huge percentage compared to some.

General Dynamics is the nation's biggest military contractor, with contracts to produce aircraft, nuclear submarines, missiles and anti-armor weapons, but Lockheed, Martin-Marietta, Raytheon, Rockwell International, McDonnell Douglas, Grumman and Fairchild are substantial suppliers as well. By way of illustration, McDonnell Douglas, which makes the DC-10, lost $60 million on commercial aircraft in 1978 but earned $230 million (pretax) on sales of its military aircraft. And Government contracts accounted for 65 percent of Lockheed's 1978 sales of $3.3 billion.

Most of the foregoing companies are likely to benefit handsomely from future defense appropriations. For example, Lockheed, Boeing and McDonnell Douglas are all in the running to build a new heavy, long-range transport capable of hauling tanks and troops as much as 6,000 miles. That contract may be worth $80 million in fiscal 1981 and $140 million the following year.

McDonnell Douglas and Fairchild will probably be major beneficiaries of the new tactical aircraft expected to be included in the new budget. Fairchild also makes tactical aircraft; its A-10 close-air-support plane is already in the Air Force Tactical Air Command. Grumman, whose 1978 aircraft and space sales totaled $1.22 billion (of $1.5 billion in consolidated sales) makes carrier-based fighters and early warning radar aircraft.

The MX mobil intercontinental ballistic missile project, one of the most expensive military projects ever, was in danger of being scuttled because of legal and environmental restrictions, but defense industry sources say Congress is likely to ease those restrictions in response to the changed political climate. TRW Inc., Martin-Marietta, Boeing, the Northrop Corporation and several other defense and technology companies are involved in the MX program.

General Dynamics, Lockheed, Litton Industries and the Ogden Corporation all own shipyards, and all are likely to benefit from President Carter's goal of increasing the fleet from fewer than 400 ships to 550 in the 1990's. The new budget is expected to include $1.7 billion for two destroyers equipped with the Aegis antiaircraft system, and it likely will contain appropriations for defense against the large Soviet submarine fleet — everything from a nuclear submarine that stalks enemy subs (built by General Dynamics) to antisubmarine warfare planes such as the Lockheed P-3 Neptune, used also by Canada, Japan, Australia, New Zealand and Iran.

An important feature of the Carter expanded defense policy is the rapid deployment force, which probably means additional helicopters, armored vehicles, weapons and ammunition. This could prove a bonanza to the Sikorsky division of United Technologies, Bell Aerospace and the FMC Corporation. The latter, for many years a manufacturer of specialized equipment for the food industry, has built thousands of tracked amphibious vehicles and now manufactures several types of armored infantry fighting vehicles.

Even the Chrysler Corporation may benefit, since it is the only American tank manufacturer. Over 20 years it has built more than 12,000 M-60 tanks, and next month the first of the Army's newest model — the faster, more mobile, turbine XM-1 — is scheduled to rumble off Chrysler assembly lines. Chrysler won $712 million in tank contracts last year. That isn't a major part of the company's total corporate sales ($13.6 billion last year), but a company official said it all helps, and added that Chrysler is capable of producing many more tanks soon after it is given the word.

Ford Aerospace and Raytheon build antiaircraft missiles, Hughes Aircraft builds antitank launchers and missiles, and General Electric and United Technologies build airplane engines. Higher defense budgets could also benefit companies not usually associated with the defense industry. Among them:

• Colt Industries, which not only makes M-16 rifles and munitions but also landing gears for military and commercial aircraft.

• The Cubic Corporation, 37 percent of whose 1978 revenues came from defense contracts primarily involving tracking, surveillance and reconnaissance systems.

• The Loral Corporation, which makes radar-jamming devices for jet fighters as well as electronics and telemetry systems for military and aerospace applications.

• The Harsco Corporation, 19 percent of whose 1978 net sales were related to such work as converting and rebuilding tactical and combat vehicles.

The parts industry should also benefit, since industry officials say many Air Force F-15 fighters (made by McDonnell Douglas) have been grounded for lack of spare engine parts. But the F-15 and F-16 fighters have also been grounded because of problems with their Pratt & Whitney-built F-100 engines that have caused frequent stalling in flight and emergency landings. Pratt & Whitney, a division of United Technologies, has redesigned and modified part of the engine, but the overhaul won't be completed until 1981.

Most of the increased defense money probably will not work its way into the nation's economy until next year because of the long lead time required for most defense projects. Some officials welcome the lag, saying that any sudden infusion of new money could strain the resources of an industry that is already so short of skilled workers that some aerospace companies pay employees $1,000 bonuses for every engineer they bring aboard.

There is also a long wait for machine tools, a development that prompted one analyst to say, "Bendix will be laughing all the way to the bank with its acquisition of Warner & Swazey," a major manufacturer of metal cutting tools. But the way things are going for the defense industry these days, Bendix better get to the bank early unless it doesn't mind standing in line.

Dayton Counting on Military

BY DOUG MCINNIS | JAN. 14, 1985

DAYTON, OHIO — Many people here think of this as a General Motors town. The General Motors Corporation's 10 big manufacturing plants dominate the industrial landscape, and G.M.'s employment levels — now more than 20,000 workers, or one out of five manufacturing jobs — are closely monitored as a gauge of the local economy.

But a number of business and academic people here are beginning to conclude that military spending may really be what makes Dayton tick. Many are counting on the military presence to provide a crucial advantage in transforming Dayton into a high-technology center. That sort of revival is badly needed to offset substantial job losses in Dayton's traditional industries. In recent years, factory jobs at such employers as G.M., the NCR Corporation and the Chrysler Corporation have fallen by more than 25,000.

CONCENTRATION OF JOBS

The military advantage comes from the presence of sprawling Wright Patterson Air Force Base, the center for research and development for the United States Air Force. With 32,000 workers, it is the largest single concentration of jobs in one site in Ohio.

The base's spending for payrolls, services and construction create a $1.6 billion a year impact on the local economy. And as defense dollars turn over, they create another 24,000 jobs locally, the Dayton area Chamber of Commerce estimated.

"I can't put too much emphasis on what Wright Patterson means to the Dayton economy," said Jerry L. Kirby, chairman of the Citizens Federal Savings and Loan Association, the state's second-largest thrift institution. Mr. Kirby is also the chairman of the Chamber of Commerce.

Local officials see even greater benefits flowing from the base as Dayton seeks a high-technology future. Although unemployment in

Dayton has exceeded the national average, it has run below the Ohio average, in part because of Wright Patterson's stabilizing presence. The latest figures, released last month, show Dayton's unemployment at 7.3 percent, compared with a state average of 8.7 percent.

BENEFITS ARE GRADUAL

To be sure, the benefits will come only gradually. It can take a decade or more for new high-technology companies to generate significant employment. Moreover, many new jobs require specialized skills that put them far out of reach of the thousands of industrial workers here whose jobs disappeared between 1979 and 1983.

But employment at the base has grown by several thousand in the last two or three years.

In impact on the Dayton economy, "I would think the Defense Department would be No. 1 and the auto industry No. 2," said John Cordrey, chief economist for the Chamber of Commerce. In years past, there was never any question that the auto industry was first.

Already, dozens of local high-technology companies, employing more than 2,000 people, owe their existence to military research contracts awarded through the base. Many of these firms have been started by former researchers at Wright Patterson, where the Air Force is developing such projects as the B-1B bomber, the Maverick missile and the F-16 fighter plane, and where advanced laboratories are developing tough new composite materials for the nation's air and space programs.

ELECTRONIC WARFARE

One example is Systems Research Laboratories Inc., which specializes in electronic warfare and other advanced military research. Since its formation in 1955 by Fritz Russ, a former engineer at Wright Patterson, Systems Research has grow to 1,000 employees and the company regularly produces spinoff companies of its own, such as Dayton General Systems Inc., which develops computer software for regulating energy use, and Autometrix Inc., which builds laser measurement gauges. "We probably have 20 companies in Dayton that are offshoots," Mr. Russ said.

Systems Research has also branched out beyond military research. For instance, it is working on the development of anti-skid braking systems for General Motors. The research is an outgrowth of Systems Research's work on aircraft braking systems.

"I would suggest that there will continue to be spinoffs" from the base, said Burnell Roberts, chairman of the Mead Corporation, the well-known paper products company that employs about 1,500.

MEAD HAS BENEFITED

The Mead Corporation itself has benefited. Mr. Roberts noted that Mead Data Central, the company's fast-growing and highly profitable subsidiary, was an outgrowth of a small defense contractor that Mead bought more than a decade ago.

Mead Data Central provides the Lexis-Nexis information retrieval service. Among other things, the small defense contractor specialized in the infant technology of computer-based information retrieval. In the years since the acquisition, Mead Data Central has grown to more than 600 employees at its Dayton headquarters.

"The base is one of the magnets that is drawing high-tech companies into Dayton," said Lieut. Col. Allan Cummings, a Wright Patterson spokesman.

REALIZED IMPORTANCE

It was not until recent years that many people here realized the importance of the base to Dayton. But as jobs slipped away at old-line companies — automotive parts, appliances, tool and die, foundry and tires — the base loomed increasingly important in Dayton's future.

To encourage defense-related companies to move to Dayton, private and public development officials are emphasizing the low housing prices and relatively cheap office-rental rates here, which remain depressed. Recent recruiting has brought in as many as 750 jobs, including the defense group of TRW Inc. The influx has helped spawn a trio of office park projects that is helping to add some one million square feet of office and manufacturing space in an emerging high-tech corridor along Interstate 675, bordering Dayton on the east.

And all of these developments are gradually helping to ease Dayton's image as a lunch-bucket industrial city, indistinguishable from its neighbors in the Middle West.

The president of Wright State University, Robert Kegerreis, who has been influential in the effort to promote technology growth here, said many people "think of Dayton in the same way they think of Youngstown — as a depressed area. That's simply not the case at all."

Fear of Lost Jobs Is Hurdle to Reining In Defense Contracts

BY CHRISTOPHER DREW | MARCH 8, 2009

IN PLEDGING LAST WEEK that the "days of giving defense contractors a blank check are over," President Obama is taking on the giant weapons contracting system that he says has "gone amok."

Nearly everyone agrees that huge cost overruns and delays in creating new weapons have become the norm. Even so, fierce battles are starting over some of the prominent programs he would like to cancel or cut back.

Defense experts say Mr. Obama will inevitably clash with members of Congress who are concerned about protecting jobs that such programs provide.

"He says he's not afraid to fight, and he's fighting on a lot of fronts," said Lawrence J. Korb, a former high-ranking Pentagon official, referring to the president's plans to reshape health care, education and energy policies.

But, Mr. Korb said, history has shown that to make lasting cuts to big weapons programs, "you need a president who says to Congress, 'Put this in there, and I'll veto it.' "

Congressional and industry leaders say they recognize that defense spending is peaking, and the time has come — given the many financial strains on the federal government — to overhaul an acquisition system that has resulted in smaller, but more expensive, fleets of combat planes and ships.

There is also broad political support for the Pentagon's plans to shift some of the more than $650 billion in defense spending from futuristic weapons programs to simpler arms that the troops in Iraq and Afghanistan can use now.

But with a labor report on Friday showing that the economy has lost 4.4 million jobs since the recession began, "if you're talking about canceling major weapons systems, that becomes hard," said William S. Cohen, a former senator from Maine who served as defense secretary under President Bill Clinton.

"Given the economic climate we're operating in now, any congressman or senator is going to say, 'I've got to protect the jobs in my district or state,' and that's understandable," Mr. Cohen said. "The difficulty now is how do you get a majority to vote against their own interests, even if you could persuade them that the changes would be best for the national defense?"

Perhaps the most controversial program in Mr. Obama's sights is the Air Force's advanced F-22 fighter jet, which the Bush administration tried for years to halt, saying it was a cold war relic. Mr. Korb and other analysts say that if the president is determined to fix the contracting process, canceling the F-22 would send a strong signal.

Lockheed Martin, which makes the plane and buys parts from more than 1,000 suppliers in 44 states, has mounted a lobbying campaign emphasizing the high-paying jobs it creates.

Forty-four senators and 200 representatives have written to Mr. Obama urging him to keep buying the planes, costing $143 million each, and some analysts think a compromise to buy 30 to 60 more could be reached.

Still, industry executives say that Mr. Obama and his defense secretary, Robert M. Gates, are clearly serious about making cuts and revamping a contracting process that has let the price tag of the 95 biggest programs grow nearly $300 billion beyond their original cost estimates.

Gordon Adams, a professor at American University in Washington, said parts of the $10 billion missile defense programs, which are still being tested, represent "low-hanging fruit" for Mr. Obama. His team might also cancel a radar-evading $3.3 billion destroyer that even the Navy says it can no longer afford. And the Army's sweeping $160 billion modernization plan seems likely to be scaled back.

Mr. Gates has said that the administration would decide by April on the cuts it plans to make. Then the action will shift to Capitol Hill, where defense contractors are likely to push back, using the jobs argument.

Some studies suggest that defense spending diverts resources from more productive investments and is a costly way to create jobs. But Marion C. Blakey, chief executive of the Aerospace Industries Association, a trade group in Washington, said most of the defense jobs are relatively high-paying and provide critical technical training.

"It's a very dangerous thing to contemplate cutting back on those jobs in this economy," Ms. Blakey said.

Lockheed Martin says 25,000 jobs depend directly on the F-22, and perhaps 70,000 more indirectly. But only a few thousand of the people working for the company or its suppliers would face immediate layoffs if the program were canceled, because production would continue for two more years under previous government orders.

Many studies, including those by the Government Accountability Office and Pentagon boards, have shown that many weapons projects start out with unrealistically low cost estimates, depend on technologies that are not ready and face constant changes in design requirements.

"The root cause is that you've got an ever-changing kaleidoscope of entities involved in the decisions, and nobody has the authority to just say no and be held accountable for it," said John F. Lehman, the first secretary of the navy in the Reagan administration. "That's what has to change."

The U.S. Still Leans on the Military-Industrial Complex

ANALYSIS | BY LOUIS UCHITELLE | SEPT. 22, 2017

IF YOU WANT TO SEE what President Trump can do to expand manufacturing in America, look past his criticism of free trade and the few jobs he may have saved at Carrier. Instead, look at his plans for the military.

Manufacturing has always relied on public funding in one form or another, and in particular on outlays for weaponry, even nearly three decades after the end of the Cold War. Roughly 10 percent of the $2.2 trillion in factory output in the United States goes into the production of weapons sold mainly to the Defense Department for use by the armed forces.

And the spending shows. The United States, after all, has 10 aircraft carriers in active service versus just one for China, although China has a bigger manufacturing industry than the United States. One can argue that China is bent on big increases in weapons production and is still in the early stages. Whatever the case, America's weapons production is still far greater than China's, while China has burnished its reputation as a manufacturer of civilian goods for export and, increasingly, for its own citizens.

The United States once went that route. In the summer of 1945, after nearly five years of wartime rationing, the civilian population of the United States was starved for new cars and appliances, new clothing and shoes, and new homes and their furnishings. So was the rest of the world, and American manufacturers prospered by meeting that need as well. Converting factories to civilian production was a no-brainer and sufficiently profitable to match wartime earnings.

After the Korean War in the early 1950s, however, a somewhat similar conversion back to civilian production wasn't as profitable. And companies that considered it in the early 1990s, like General

Dynamics in Groton, Conn., decided to stick with making weapons for the Defense Department. These companies argued — accurately — that military work was more profitable and, in those days, generated more jobs.

As weapons production increased, the manufacture of autos and electronics shifted partly or wholly overseas. So did the production of other civilian products — leaving behind weapons bought by the Defense Department as an ever bigger share of the nation's factory output.

While President Dwight D. Eisenhower warned of the perils of the "military-industrial complex" in his farewell address in January 1961, the Vietnam War accentuated this reliance on weapons production, which became embedded in annual budgets. That may well continue in the years ahead. In his first budget proposal in May, Mr. Trump called for significant cuts in domestic spending but roughly a 10 percent increase in military outlays.

Given the history of recent decades, is it any wonder that we now have a president who, at least in part, equates "making America strong again" with an enhanced military equipped with the weaponry that an enhanced military requires?

Public money flows to factory owners in many ways — often as a result of the frequent bidding by municipal governments to persuade a manufacturer to locate a factory in one community rather than another. These auctions sometimes top $100 million per factory location.

A manufacturer who finally accepts a municipality's bid collects tax breaks, a gift of land on which to put a factory and sometimes the cost of building and equipping the factory itself at taxpayers' expense. Cities and towns are that eager to have a factory, with its network of nearby suppliers and its relatively well-paying jobs — relative, that is, to the lower paying retail and service industry work that is often the alternative for high-school- or even junior-college-educated men and women.

That outlay of taxpayer money is concentrated in eight sectors of manufacturing, including ammunition, aircraft, guided missiles, shipbuilding and armored vehicles. Shut down production in those areas and factory production in America, measured as value added, would shrink 10 percent or more, according to Richard Aboulafia, a vice president of the Teal Group, a defense consulting firm.

Mr. Aboulafia based his estimate, he said, on an analysis of the Defense Department budget and export data. Dan Luria, research director of the Michigan Manufacturing Technology Center, concurred with those figures. To put the matter graphically, factories in the United States churn out one rifle barrel for every nine auto fenders.

Cutting back on factory production isn't the direction the Trump administration has been going. Instead, the promise is that — whatever goods they produce — the Trump era's factories will be big employers. But the reality is that modern factories, even when they materialize, are highly automated, which helps to explain why the manufacturing work force has bumped along at less than 13 million for nearly a decade, according to the Labor Department, although factory output — including weapons production — keeps rising smartly.

These constraints make me yearn for the good old days just after World War 11, when America seemed to have easier policy choices. Even inexpensive trinkets were manufactured in America, and my mother, for one, ordered her children to stay away from a neighborhood boy whose parents had bought him a BB gun. Disarmament ran deep in the late 1940s. We didn't need to produce weapons, even BB guns, to keep manufacturing afloat. I'm afraid that we do now.

LOUIS UCHITELLE covered economics for The New York Times for more than 20 years. This essay is drawn from his latest book, "Making It: Why Manufacturing Still Matters," published in May by the New Press.

Blackwater's Rich Contracts

EDITORIAL | BY THE NEW YORK TIMES | OCT. 3, 2007

IT SHOULD COME as no surprise that the Bush administration would take any opportunity to reward its political friends with lavish no-bid contracts. Still, there is something particularly unseemly about the munificent payments to Blackwater, the State Department's principal private security contractor in Iraq.

With many Iraqis still seething after Blackwater guards killed as many as 17 people two weeks ago, it is evident that Blackwater and other security contractors are undermining the military's efforts to win over Iraqis.

Now an investigation by the House Committee on Oversight and Government Reform has underscored the lavish extent of Blackwater's payments and its relationship to the Bush administration. The committee, which held hearings on the use of security contractors in Iraq yesterday, should investigate these links further.

Former Bush administration officials are peppered throughout Blackwater's highest executive positions. Erik Prince, the former Navy Seal who founded the company, was a White House intern under President George H. W. Bush and has been a Republican financier since, with more than $225,000 in political contributions.

Mr. Prince's sister, Betsy DeVos, is a former chairwoman of the Michigan Republican Party and a "pioneer" who raised $100,000 for the Bush-Cheney ticket in 2004. Her husband, the former Amway chief executive Richard DeVos Jr., was the Republican nominee for governor of Michigan in 2006.

Mr. Prince denied yesterday that his connections had anything to do with it, but he certainly has done well under the Bush administration. Federal contracts account for about 90 percent of the revenue of Prince Group holdings, of which Blackwater is a subsidiary. Since 2001, when it made less than $1 million in federal contracts, Blackwater has received more than $1 billion in such contracts — including at least one with the State Department for hundreds of millions of dollars that was awarded without open, competitive bidding.

The Congressional investigation found that Blackwater charges the government $1,222 per day for each private military operative — more than six times the wage of an equivalent soldier. And still it uncovered instances of overcharging. It reported that an audit in 2005 by the State Department's inspector general found Blackwater was charging separately for "drivers" and "security specialists" who were, in fact, the same people.

The fallout from Blackwater's heavy-handed tactics is a reminder of the folly of using a private force to perform military missions in a war zone. These jobs need to be brought back into government hands as soon as practicable, and remaining private contractors placed under the jurisdiction of military law.

Henry Waxman, the California Democrat who is chairman of the oversight committee, said yesterday that if private contractors are meant to provide security on the cheap, it's not working. "It's costing us more money," he said, "and I believe it's costing us problems." Blackwater's contracts should spur Congress to further investigate the Bush administration's practice of using Iraq to slip rich deals to its friends.

30 False Fronts Won Contracts for Blackwater

BY JAMES RISEN AND MARK MAZZETTI | SEPT. 3, 2010

WASHINGTON — Blackwater Worldwide created a web of more than 30 shell companies or subsidiaries in part to obtain millions of dollars in American government contracts after the security company came under intense criticism for reckless conduct in Iraq, according to Congressional investigators and former Blackwater officials.

While it is not clear how many of those businesses won contracts, at least three had deals with the United States military or the Central Intelligence Agency, according to former government and company officials. Since 2001, the intelligence agency has awarded up to $600 million in classified contracts to Blackwater and its affiliates, according to a United States government official.

The Senate Armed Services Committee this week released a chart that identified 31 affiliates of Blackwater, now known as Xe Services. The network was disclosed as part of a committee's investigation into government contracting. The investigation revealed the lengths to which Blackwater went to continue winning contracts after Blackwater guards killed 17 Iraqi civilians in Baghdad in September 2007. That episode and other reports of abuses led to criminal and Congressional investigations, and cost the company its lucrative security contract with the State Department in Iraq.

The network of companies — which includes several businesses located in offshore tax havens — allowed Blackwater to obscure its involvement in government work from contracting officials or the public, and to assure a low profile for any of its classified activities, said former Blackwater officials, who, like the government officials, spoke only on condition of anonymity.

Senator Carl Levin, the Michigan Democrat who is chairman of the Armed Services Committee, said in a statement that it was worth "looking into why Blackwater would need to create the dozens of other names" and said he had requested that the Justice Department investigate whether Blackwater officers misled the government when using subsidiaries to solicit contracts.

The C.I.A.'s continuing relationship with the company, which recently was awarded a $100 million contract to provide security at agency bases in Afghanistan, has drawn harsh criticism from some members of Congress, who argue that the company's tarnished record should preclude it from such work. At least two of the Blackwater-affiliated companies, XPG and Greystone, obtained secret contracts from the agency, according to interviews with a half dozen former Blackwater officials.

A C.I.A. spokesman, Paul Gimigliano, said that Xe's current duties for the agency were to provide security for agency operatives. Contractors "do the tasks we ask them to do in strict accord with the law; they are supervised by C.I.A. staff officers; and they are held to the highest standards of conduct" he said. "As for Xe specifically, they help provide security in tough environments, an assignment at which their people have shown both skill and courage."

Congress began to investigate the affiliated companies last year, after the shooting deaths of two Afghans by Blackwater security personnel working for a subsidiary named Paravant, which had obtained Pentagon contracts in Afghanistan. In a Senate hearing earlier this year, Army officials said that when they awarded the contract to Paravant for training of the Afghan Army, they had no idea that the business was part of Blackwater.

While Congressional investigators have identified other Blackwater-linked businesses, it was not the focus of their inquiry to determine how much money from government contracts flowed through the web of corporations, especially money earmarked for clandestine programs. The former company officials say that Greystone did extensive work for the intelligence community, though they did not describe the nature of the activities. The firm was incorporated in Barbados for tax purposes, but had executives who worked at Blackwater's headquarters in North Carolina.

The former company officials say that Erik Prince, the business's founder, was eager to find ways to continue to handle secret work after the 2007 shootings in Baghdad's Nisour Square and set up a special office to handle classified work at his farm in Middleburg, Va.

Enrique Prado, a former top C.I.A. official who joined the contractor, worked closely with Mr. Prince to develop Blackwater's clandestine abilities, according to several former officials. In an internal e-mail obtained by The New York Times, Mr. Prado claimed that he had created a Blackwater spy network that could be hired by the American government.

"We have a rapidly growing, worldwide network of folks that can do everything from surveillance to ground truth to disruption operations," Mr. Prado wrote in the October 2007 message, in which he asked another Blackwater official whether the Drug Enforcement Administration might be interested in using the spy network. "These are all foreign nationals," he added, "so deniability is built in and should be a big plus."

It is not clear whether Mr. Prado's secret spy service ever conducted any operations for the government. From 2004 to 2006, both Mr. Prado and Mr. Prince were involved in a C.I.A. program to hunt senior leaders of Al Qaeda that had been outsourced to Blackwater, though current and former American officials said that the assassination program did not carry out any operations. Company employees also loaded bombs and missiles onto Predator drones in Pakistan, work that was terminated last year by the C.I.A.

Both Mr. Prince and Mr. Prado declined to be interviewed for this article.

The company is facing a string of legal problems, including the indictment in April of five former Blackwater officials on weapons and obstruction charges, and civil suits stemming from the 2007 shootings in Iraq.

The business is up for sale by Mr. Prince, who colleagues say is embittered by the public criticism and scrutiny that Blackwater has faced. He has not been implicated in the criminal charges against his former subordinates, but he has recently moved his family to Abu Dhabi, where he hopes to focus on obtaining contracts from governments in Africa and the Middle East, according to colleagues and former company officials.

After awarding Blackwater the new security contract in June, the C.I.A. director, Leon E. Panetta, publicly defended the decision, saying Blackwater had "cleaned up its act."

But Rep. Jan Schakowsky, an Illinois Democrat and a member of the House Intelligence Committee, said she could not understand why the intelligence community had been unwilling to cut ties to Blackwater. "I am continually and increasingly mystified by this relationship," she said. "To engage with a company that is such a chronic, repeat offender, it's reckless."

It is unclear how much of Blackwater's relationship with the C.I.A. will become public during the criminal proceedings in North Carolina because the Obama administration won a court order limiting the use of classified information. Among other things, company executives are accused of obtaining large numbers of AK-47s and M-4 automatic weapons, but arranging to make it appear as if they had been bought by the sheriff's department in Camden County, N.C. Such purchases were legal only if made by law enforcement agencies.

But defense lawyers say they hope to argue that Blackwater had a classified contract with the C.I.A. and wanted at least some of the guns for weapons training for agency officers.

Reining In Soldiers of Fortune

OPINION | BY SEAN MCFATE | APRIL 17, 2015

WASHINGTON — Ten years ago, I found myself in Burundi, sipping a Coke with the country's president, the American ambassador and the president's 8-year-old daughter. The president's life was in danger, and the American government sent me in to keep him alive.

The Rwandan genocide had begun in 1994 after the presidents of Burundi and Rwanda were assassinated. In 2004, an extremist Hutu group planned on assassinating the new president of Burundi to reignite it. My job was to prevent this from happening.

I wasn't a member of the C.I.A. or a covert military unit. I was a "contractor" ("mercenary" to some), working for a company called DynCorp International. This is increasingly how foreign policy is enacted today.

I'm proud of the work I did as a contractor in Africa, but my buddies from the United States Army's 82nd Airborne Division, in which I had once served, scowled that I had "gone mercenary" and was lost to "the dark side." A fellow graduate student at Harvard accused me of being "morally promiscuous." Yet the work was similar to what I did in the military, and the pay and benefits weren't that great, despite perceptions to the contrary.

Private military contractors are back in the news after four former Blackwater guards were sentenced to 30 years to life in prison. In 2007, they killed 17 innocent Iraqis in Baghdad. They mistook civilians for terrorists and murdered them. It was wrong. Many around the world have hailed their long prison sentences as a victory for America and Iraq.

But fewer people remember the Haditha massacre of 2005, when a squad of United States Marines murdered 24 innocent Iraqis in a revenge killing spree. It started when one of their Humvees hit an improvised mine, killing one and injuring two more. The squad immediately killed five people in the street. They then went house to house, and killed 19 more civilians, ranging in age from 3 to 76. Many were shot multiple times at close range, some still in their pajamas. One was in a wheelchair.

The military investigated and acquitted the Marines, except one who got a slap on the wrist. The Pentagon blamed the affair on "an unscrupulous enemy" and dismissed it as a "case study" that illustrates "how simple failures can lead to disastrous results."

Like the Blackwater guards, the Marines committed atrocities. But the outcomes were different. For the Marines, there was a single internal investigation, and the charges were quietly dropped. By contrast, Blackwater's crime immediately sparked international ire and multiple high-level inquiries. It remains seared in the global imagination as a nadir of the Iraq War. Those contractors will spend most of their lives behind bars; the Marines of Haditha will not.

There have been other abuses, from Abu Ghraib to civilian deaths from air strikes. So far, no American official has been sent to jail for 30 years. The United States seems to hold armed contractors to a higher ethical standard than its own armed forces.

America turned to the private sector for personnel that its all-volunteer military could not muster. In Iraq half of the personnel in war zones were contracted, and in Afghanistan it was closer to 70 percent. America may fight future wars mainly with contractors.

Now others are following America's lead. Nigeria hired hundreds of mercenaries to fight Boko Haram. Russia is allegedly using them in Ukraine. And oil companies and humanitarian organizations are turning to private military companies to protect their workers and property in dangerous places, and there is an argument that the United Nations should use this industry to augment thinning peace-keeping missions.

Private force isn't a new phenomenon. Contract warfare was the norm in the Middle Ages. Like today, for-profit warriors were called condottiere ("contractor" in old Italian). They usually fought for the highest bidders: kings, city-states, rich families, even popes.

The problems associated with private force were solved when states began monopolizing the market and put mercenaries out of business. They created large national armies accountable to governments and bonded by patriotism, rather than cash. This process took centuries, but is now unraveling.

Few would welcome a new unbridled market for force, yet it is already developing. The industry continues to proliferate as new consumers seek security in a deeply insecure world. And mercenaries are less expensive than standing armies, just like renting a car is cheaper than owning one. The Congressional Budget Office found in 2008 that Blackwater cost 10 percent less than a comparable army unit in wartime Iraq, and a private force costs nothing in peacetime because its contract can be terminated.

The question now is how to minimize the risks of private armies. Some companies have proposed self-regulation, but that proposal lacks teeth and is dependent on firms confessing their own crimes, which is bad for business. Nor can it be externally regulated; strict laws will only drive these firms offshore or underground.

The solution is to use market power. Superclients, like the United States or the United Nations, could shape best practices by rewarding good firms with profitable contracts and withholding them from bad firms. America or the U.N. could establish a licensing and registration regime that all industry members must observe in order to be eligible for contracts. This would include clear standards for training and vetting members and transparent mechanisms for oversight and accountability.

Multibillion dollar industries don't just evaporate, and outlawing private security forces won't work. Relying on the market is the best way to avoid a return to the medieval chaos of armies for hire.

SEAN MCFATE is a senior fellow at the Atlantic Council and author of "The Modern Mercenary: Private Armies and What They Mean for World Order."

CHAPTER 4

A New Era of War and National Defense

A perennial refrain in the military spending debate goes like this: Warfare in the future will be smaller, lighter and more distributed. Therefore, military spending could be streamlined, focusing not on projects like giant submarines or tanks, but on lighter, cheaper and more mass-produced weapons systems. While this makes some sense on the face of it, the politics and profits of defense spending can often get in the way of reason and accountability.

National Defense: Against What?

EDITORIAL | BY THE NEW YORK TIMES | JAN. 8, 1990

IT WON'T BE ENOUGH. In the 1991 budget about to go to Congress, the Administration will probably propose a cut of only $6 billion in military spending. The President and Defense Secretary Cheney will have to make deeper cuts. As the Soviet threat recedes, Congress will press to reduce the deficit and spend more for domestic needs.

Can the Administration respond realistically? Yes, but to avoid chopping haphazardly, its cuts will have to be guided by a new defense policy, one that reassesses threats for the 1990's and provides the forces needed to meet them.

A Soviet invasion of Western Europe was long believed to be the gravest military threat to America's security. Particularly menacing were Soviet forces in East Germany and Czechoslovakia, poised to mobilize and attack on short notice. That threat has kept 300,000 U.S. troops in West Germany and required others to remain on active duty back home, ready to be airlifted to Europe.

But now, six divisions of Soviet troops and tanks are withdrawing from Eastern Europe. The Warsaw Pact lacks military cohesion. U.S. intelligence has lowered its assessment of Soviet military readiness and thinks the U.S. will have at least a month's warning of attack.

As a result, fewer U.S. troops need remain in Europe. Those at home could be transported to the Continent in ships instead of planes. And the military could rely on reserves instead of active-duty troops. All these steps would save money.

Meanwhile, as the Soviet threat recedes, lesser contingencies loom larger, like instability in Eastern Europe and the third world. But the foreseeable force requirements do not call, any more than interventions on the scale of Panama, for large standing armies. They do call for mobility — smaller, more transportable forces, with equipment stored at pre-positioned sites or aboard ship. Most of this capability is already on hand. It's hard to see why the Pentagon needs all the attack aircraft or carrier battle groups now planned.

The decline in Soviet defense spending and military modernization allows a shift in the pace of Pentagon modernization, from replacing to upgrading some weapons and canceling others. Arleigh Burke class destroyers bristling with missiles and sophisticated electronics seem technologically excessive for today's threats. So do new attack helicopters and stealth fighter planes.

The slowdown in Soviet nuclear modernization provides an even more compelling opportunity for savings. Mr. Bush and Mr. Cheney can save at least $30 billion by cutting back research on Star Wars and antisatellite weapons. They can save billions more by buying one new mobile land-based missile instead of two. By building six B-2 bombers for flight testing, and no more, they can save $30 billion more over five years.

Cuts like these made gradually over a decade could halve the defense budget without harming national security.

But Mr. Cheney's first response to the new strategic and political environment has been largely cosmetic. He doesn't propose an actual reduction in 1991 outlays at all; he proposes an increase over the current fiscal year, though not by as much as previously planned. He's also contemplating $180 billion less in spending from 1992 through 1994. Even that won't mean budgets much below the current level. It would be a reduction only from the unrealistic $320 billion-plus a year his predecessor projected. More Pentagon belt-tightening like that won't save enough, particularly if the belt's elastic.

To save real money, Mr. Bush and Mr. Cheney have to make choices and eliminate programs.

Panetta to Offer Strategy for Cutting Military Budget

BY ELISABETH BUMILLER AND THOM SHANKER | JAN. 2, 2012

WASHINGTON — Defense Secretary Leon E. Panetta is set this week to reveal his strategy that will guide the Pentagon in cutting hundreds of billions of dollars from its budget, and with it the Obama administration's vision of the military that the United States needs to meet 21st-century threats, according to senior officials.

In a shift of doctrine driven by fiscal reality and a deal last summer that kept the United States from defaulting on its debts, Mr. Panetta is expected to outline plans for carefully shrinking the military — and in so doing make it clear that the Pentagon will not maintain the ability to fight two sustained ground wars at once.

Instead, he will say that the military will be large enough to fight and win one major conflict, while also being able to "spoil" a second adversary's ambitions in another part of the world while conducting a number of other smaller operations, like providing disaster relief or enforcing a no-flight zone.

Pentagon officials, in the meantime, are in final deliberations about potential cuts to virtually every important area of military spending: the nuclear arsenal, warships, combat aircraft, salaries, and retirement and health benefits. With the war in Iraq over and the one in Afghanistan winding down, Mr. Panetta is weighing how significantly to shrink America's ground forces.

There is broad agreement on the left, right and center that $450 billion in cuts over a decade — the amount that the White House and Pentagon agreed to last summer — is acceptable. That is about 8 percent of the Pentagon's base budget. But there is intense debate about an additional $500 billion in cuts that may have to be made if Congress follows through with deeper reductions.

Mr. Panetta and defense hawks say a reduction of $1 trillion, about

17 percent of the Pentagon's base budget, would be ruinous to national security. Democrats and a few Republicans say that it would be painful but manageable; they add that there were steeper military cuts after the Cold War and the wars in Korea and Vietnam.

"Even at a trillion dollars, this is a shallower build-down than any of the last three we've done," said Gordon Adams, who oversaw military budgets in the Clinton White House and is now a fellow at the Stimson Center, a nonprofit research group in Washington. "It would still be the world's most dominant military. We would be in an arms race with ourselves."

Many who are more worried about cuts, including Mr. Panetta, acknowledge that Pentagon personnel costs are unsustainable and that generous retirement benefits may have to be scaled back to save crucial weapons programs.

"If we allow the current trend to continue," said Arnold L. Punaro, a consultant on a Pentagon advisory group, the Defense Business Board, who has pushed for changes in the military retirement system, "we're going to turn the Department of Defense into a benefits company that occasionally kills a terrorist."

Mr. Panetta will outline the strategy guiding his spending plans at a news conference this week, and the specific cuts — for now, the Pentagon has prepared about $260 billion in cuts for the next five years — will be detailed in the president's annual budget submission to Congress, where they will be debated and almost certainly amended before approval. Although the proposals look to budget cuts over a decade, any future president can decide to propose an alternative spending plan to Congress.

The looming cuts inevitably force decisions on the scope and future of the American military. If, say, the Pentagon saves $7 billion over a decade by reducing the number of aircraft carriers to 10 from 11, would there be sufficient forces in the Pacific to counter an increasingly bold China? If the Pentagon saves nearly $150 billion in the next 10 years by shrinking the Army to, say, 483,000 troops from

570,000, would America be prepared for a grinding, lengthy ground war in Asia?

What about saving more than $100 billion in health care cutbacks for working-age military retirees? Would that break a promise to those who risked their lives for the country?

The calculations exclude the costs of the wars in Iraq and Afghanistan, which will go down over the next decade. Even after the winding down of the wars and the potential $1 trillion in cuts over the next decade, the Pentagon's annual budget, now $530 billion, would shrink to $472 billion in 2013, or about the size of the budget in 2007.

It is also important to remember that Mr. Panetta, a former White House budget chief, understands budget politics like few other defense secretaries. When he sent a dire letter to Capitol Hill late last year that held out the prospect of huge reductions in some of Congress's favorite weapons programs, analysts saw it as a classic tactic to rouse the Hill to his side.

They noted that Mr. Panetta did not cite the $100 billion that the previous defense secretary, Robert M. Gates, said could be saved by reducing the number of contractors, cutting overhead, consolidating technology and limiting spending in the executive offices of the Pentagon.

"Talking about business practices doesn't sound the alarm bells," said Travis Sharp, a defense budget specialist at the Center for a New American Security, a defense policy research institution.

Here is a look at other areas for reductions:

Military benefits and salaries, although politically difficult to cut, are first in the line of sight of many defense budget analysts. Scaling back the Pentagon's health care and retirement systems and capping raises would yield hundreds of billions of dollars in projected savings over the next decade.

As it stands now, the Pentagon spends $181 billion each year, nearly a third of its base budget, on military personnel costs: $107 billion for salaries and allowances, $50 billion for health care and $24 billion in retirement pay.

Kentucky National Guard troops in Baghdad.

One independent analyst, Todd Harrison of the Center for Strategic and Budgetary Assessments, a nonpartisan policy and research group in Washington, has calculated that if military personnel costs continue rising at the rate they have over the past decade, and overall Pentagon spending does not increase, by 2039 the entire defense budget would be consumed by personnel costs.

Most of Washington's "cut lists" recommend increases in fees for beneficiaries in the Pentagon's health insurance, Tricare. But the higher fees would affect only working-age retirees and not active-duty personnel, who do not pay for health care.

Other proposals call for capping increases in military salaries, which have had double-digit increases since the Sept. 11 attacks, often because Congress gave the troops raises beyond those requested by the Pentagon.

The chief target for weapons cuts is the F-35 Joint Strike Fighter, one of the most expensive weapons programs in history. The Pentagon has plans to spend nearly $400 billion to buy 2,500 of the stealth jets through 2035, but reductions are expected.

The debate centers on how necessary the advanced stealth fighter really is and whether missions could be carried out with the less expensive F-16s. The main advantage of the F-35 is its ability to evade radar systems, making it difficult to shoot down — an attribute that is important only if the United States anticipates a war with another technologically advanced military.

"It would matter some with Iran, it would matter a lot with China," said Michael E. O'Hanlon, a defense analyst at the Brookings Institution and the author of a recent book, "The Wounded Giant: America's Armed Forces in an Age of Austerity."

Nowhere is balancing budget and strategy more challenging than in deciding how large a ground combat force the nation needs and can afford. The Army chief of staff, Gen. Ray Odierno, the former commander in Iraq, points out that the Army had 480,000 people in uniform before the Sept. 11 attacks, and at that number was supposed to be able to fight two wars at once.

But the Army proved to be too small to sustain the wars in Afghanistan and Iraq and was increased to its current size of 570,000. The Army is now set to drop to 520,000 soldiers, beginning in 2015, although few expect that to be the floor. The reality is that the United States may not be able to afford waging two wars at once.

"That said, there are certain risks with falling off the two-war posture," said Andrew F. Krepinevich Jr., a military expert at the Center for Strategic and Budgetary Assessments. "You may risk losing the confidence of some allies, and you may risk emboldening your adversaries. But at the end of the day, a strategy of bluffing, or asserting that you have a capability that you don't, is probably the worst posture of all."

Studies by the Center for a New American Security, the Sustainable Defense Task Force and the Cato Institute, which represent a spectrum of views on defense spending, estimate that the savings from cutting the ground force could range from $41 billion by reducing the Army to 482,400 and the Marine Corps to 175,000 (from its present size of 202,000) all the way up to $387 billion if the Army drops to 360,000 and the Marines to 145,000. The final numbers will make it clear that the United States could not carry out lengthy stability and nation-building efforts, like those ordered for Afghanistan and Iraq, without a huge mobilization of the National Guard and the Reserves.

The size of the military is determined not only to win wars, but also to deter adversaries from starting hostilities. That underpins the American rationale for maintaining a combat presence at overseas bases and for conducting regular air and sea patrols around the globe. With austerity looming, those, too, might be curtailed to save money.

Senator Tom Coburn, Republican of Oklahoma, advocates saving $69.5 billion over 10 years by reducing by one-third the number of American military personnel stationed in Europe and Asia.

"This option would leave plenty of military capability by maintaining strategic air bases and naval ports to provide logistics links," Mr. Coburn wrote in a report on his budget proposals. Many Congressional budget experts also see ways to save billions of dollars by consolidating Defense Department facilities, schools and installations.

One of the largest expenses the Pentagon faces is to replace its aging strategic nuclear forces. While America's nuclear warheads are relatively inexpensive to maintain on a day-to-day basis, all three legs of the nuclear triad that deliver the punch — submarines, bombers and ground-based missiles — are reaching the end of their service life at just about the same time.

"The world has changed," said Stephen W. Young, a senior analyst with the Union of Concerned Scientists, a nuclear watchdog group. "The United States can be more than secure with a far smaller arsenal than what we currently have."

Pentagon Tries to Counter Cheap, Potent Weapons

BY THOM SHANKER | JAN. 9, 2012

WASHINGTON — President Obama's new military strategy has focused fresh attention on an increasingly important threat: the use of inexpensive weapons like mines and cyberattacks that aim not to defeat the American military in battle but to keep it at a distance.

The president and his national security team predict that the security challenges of the coming decade will be defined by this threat, just as the last one was defined by terrorism and insurgency.

A growing number of nations whose forces are overmatched by the United States are fielding these weapons, which can slow, disrupt and perhaps even halt an American offensive. Modern war plans can become mired in a bog of air defenses, mines, missiles, electronic jamming and computer-network attacks meant to degrade American advantages in technology and hardware.

It is a lesson that potential enemies drew from the way American public support for the wars in Iraq and Afghanistan plummeted as armored vehicles — each costing millions of dollars — were broken and their troops killed and maimed by roadside bombs costing only a few hundred dollars apiece.

China and Iran were identified as the countries that were leading the pursuit of "asymmetric means" to counter American military force, according to the new strategy document, which cautioned that these relatively inexpensive measures were spreading to terrorist and guerrilla cells.

At his announcement at the Pentagon last week, Mr. Obama said the country should invest in "the ability to operate in environments where adversaries try to deny us access."

The new strategy specifically orders that efforts to counter the threat, which the military calls "anti-access, area-denial," become one of the 10 primary missions of the American military. That will help define how the four armed services compete for shares of a shrinking Pentagon budget.

"The United States must maintain its ability to project power in areas in which our access and freedom to operate are challenged," the strategy document said.

"Sophisticated adversaries will use asymmetric capabilities, to include electronic and cyberwarfare, ballistic and cruise missiles, advanced air defenses, mining and other methods to complicate our operational calculus."

For example, in recent exercises by the naval arm of the Revolutionary Guards, Iran has practiced "swarming" attacks by a number of small, fast boats that could be loaded with high explosives; if one such boat got through, it might blast a hole in the hull of a major American warship.

"Iran's navy — especially the naval arm of Iran's Revolutionary Guards — has invested in vessels and armaments that are well suited to asymmetric warfare, rather than the sort of ship-to-ship conflict that Iran would surely lose," Michael Singh, managing director of the Washington Institute for Near East Policy, wrote in a recent essay for Foreign Policy.

With Chinese and Russian help, Mr. Singh added, Iran is also fielding sophisticated mines, midget submarines and mobile antiship cruise missiles.

Nathan Freier, a senior fellow at the Center for Strategic and International Studies, said, "Iran's capabilities are best suited for imposing high costs on those who might need to force their way through the Strait of Hormuz, and on those in the region whom the Iranians perceive as being complicit in enabling foreign access."

The potential challenge from China is even more significant, according to analysts. China has a fleet of diesel-electric attack submarines, which can operate quietly and effectively in waters near China's shore to threaten foreign warships. China also fields short-, medium- and long-range missiles that could put warships at risk, and has layers of radar and surface-to-air missiles along its coast.

Finding, identifying and striking an American warship is a complex military operation. But the thicket of Chinese defenses could oblige an American aircraft carrier and its strike group to operate hundreds of miles farther out to sea, decreasing the number of attack sorties its aircraft could mount in a day and diminishing their effectiveness.

Perhaps most worrisome is China's focus on electronic warfare and computer-network attacks, which might blunt the accuracy of advanced American munitions guided by satellite.

To counter these threats, the Air Force and Navy set up an office to develop complementary tactics and weaponry for what they are calling air-sea battle.

One idea is to attack an outer ring of enemy air defenses with F-35 Joint Strike Fighters, opening an alley for an F-22 stealth jet carrying sensitive surveillance pods to fly deeper into contested territory, where it could, for example, guide a powerful sea-launched cruise missile to a mobile or hidden target.

According to Lt. Gen. Herbert J. Carlisle, the Air Force deputy chief of staff for operations, plans and requirements, American computer warfare techniques could be used to spoil an adversary's decision-making process. "If we can give them bad information, or we can make them doubt the good information they have," he said.

Vice Adm. Bruce W. Clingan, the Navy's deputy chief for operations, plans and strategy, said the military was carefully studying anti-access, area-denial techniques to pinpoint potential weaknesses in an adversary's ability to identify and strike American targets.

"Do you take out his ability to shoot? Do you take him out once he's shot? Do you deny him accuracy once the missile is airborne and then you create a greater 'miss distance'?" Admiral Clingan said. "You have to work your way across that entire effect chain and how you're going to do those things to keep those missiles from threatening you."

Gen. Martin E. Dempsey, the chairman of the Joint Chiefs of Staff, will soon release his concept for operating in an anti-access, area-denial environment. The 65-page directive will identify 30 capabilities that the armed forces will need to carry out missions across contested battlefields.

New Strategy, Old Pentagon Budget

EDITORIAL | BY THE NEW YORK TIMES | JAN. 29, 2012

THE $259 BILLION in budget cuts over the next five years announced by the Pentagon may sound like a lot. But they are mainly a scaling back of previously projected spending — the delights of the Washington budget games.

This year, Pentagon spending will total $531 billion. In 2017, it will rise to $567 billion. Factoring in inflation, that amounts to only a minuscule 1.6 percent real cut. (Both numbers exclude war spending — $115 billion this year.)

After a decade of unrestrained Pentagon spending increases, President Obama deserves credit for putting on the brakes. The cuts are a credible down payment on his pledge to reduce projected defense spending by $487 billion in the next decade. They are not going to be enough. In the likely absence of a bipartisan budget pact, a further automatic across-the-board 10-year cut of nearly $500 billion is to take effect starting next January.

Even if a last-minute deal heads that off, the country needs to find more savings. And there is still plenty of room to cut deeper without jeopardizing national security.

Early in January, President Obama outlined a new, more pragmatic defense strategy. Republicans predictably claimed he was hollowing out the force — but a smarter, more restrained use of force is just what the country needs to secure its vital interests.

Much of the savings will come from cutting the size of the Army and Marine Corps by almost 13 percent and stretching out purchases of planes and ships. At the same time, the military will buy more unpiloted drones, add special operations units, equip submarines to carry more cruise missiles and expand its cyberwarfare capacities.

That makes sense in a world where terrorism and unconventional attacks are a primary threat. Any plan to downsize ground forces must be matched by a credible plan to quickly build them up, if necessary.

The Pentagon also proposes a new round of domestic base closings, a less generous formula for military pay raises after 2015 and higher health insurance premiums for military retirees (families of working-age retirees now pay $500 annually), all of which we strongly support.

Unfortunately, that new thinking has been dragged down by some old-style budgetary inertia. Mr. Obama needs to push the Pentagon to do better. Here are some additional cuts that make sense:

SHRINK THE F-35 PROGRAM The total order of stealth fighters should be reduced to 1,000, from 2,440, saving more than $150 billion. The F-35 was designed as a low-cost, supercapable aircraft. It has become the costliest Pentagon procurement project ever and its performance has been disappointing. The Air Force, Navy and Marines need to cut their losses. Most of the savings would not come until the 2020s. Over $20 billion could be saved this decade by canceling the troubled Marine Corps variant.

CUT THE NUCLEAR BUDGET Mr. Obama has declared his commitment to arms control, but there is no reflection of that in the budget plan. He needs to back it up with significant cuts in the number of deployed strategic nuclear weapons, ballistic missile submarines and intercontinental ballistic missiles. Senator Tom Coburn, a Republican, offers a sensible plan to do that, and estimates that it could save $79 billion over the next decade.

GO TO 10 AIRCRAFT CARRIER GROUPS The Pentagon could save $4 billion to $8 billion over a decade by revisiting the president's unwise decision not to eliminate one of the 11 aircraft carriers with associated ships and aircraft. Ten would provide more than enough surge capacity to support naval air operations anywhere in the world.

We know that it is politically easier to continue programs that outlive their usefulness or outrun their cost estimates — especially when Republican politicians are so eager to promise the Pentagon a blank check. And especially when the defense industry and its lobbyists are spreading so much cash around on Capitol Hill. But the country cannot afford to continue on this way. And there is no strategic argument for doing so. The era of hard choices at the Pentagon has barely begun.

Modernizing the Military, With a Technological Edge

LETTER | THE NEW YORK TIMES | FEB. 6, 2012

TO THE EDITOR:

YOUR JAN. 30 editorial "New Strategy, Old Pentagon Budget," arguing in favor of halving the F-35 Joint Strike Fighter program, reflects the wrongheaded thinking that we can cut next-generation military capabilities while simultaneously trimming troop strength. This thinking belies the fact that success and survival on the ground and on the sea require dominance in the air.

As our military shrinks in size, maintaining a technological edge is crucial. Military success depends on superior military technologies to deter some enemies and decisively defeat others.

In the last 10 years, the military has postponed replacing or upgrading many decades-old aircraft and ships. Meanwhile, Russia and China are both building fifth-generation stealth aircraft, and China is also developing an aircraft carrier fleet. These countries hope that we will sit out yet another wave of modernization, allowing them to catch up.

My former boss, Defense Secretary Robert M. Gates, said he'd "rather have a smaller, but superbly capable military than a larger, hollow, less capable one." He was right, and The Times is wrong in proposing cuts that would result in both fewer troops and less capability. That's a recipe to encourage our adversaries and weaken the foundations of our freedoms.

GORDON ENGLAND
Fort Worth, Jan. 31, 2012
The writer served as deputy secretary of defense
under President George W. Bush.

Budget Documents Detail Extent of U.S. Cyberoperations

BY DAVID E. SANGER | AUG. 31, 2013

WASHINGTON — Newly disclosed budget documents for America's intelligence agencies show how aggressively the United States is now conducting offensive cyberoperations against other nations, even as the Obama administration protests attacks on American computer networks by China, Iran and Russia.

The documents, obtained by The Washington Post from Edward J. Snowden, the former National Security Agency contractor, and described by the paper in its Saturday editions, indicate 231 such operations in 2011, a year after the first evidence emerged of an American- and Israeli-led cyberattack against Iran's nuclear-enrichment center.

That number suggests that President Obama was not deterred by the disclosure of the Iranian operation, which became evident because of a technological error, and is pressing ahead on using cyberweapons against a variety of targets.

The Post did not publish the documents. Last week, it said it had withheld most of the 178 pages of documents at the request of government officials because of the sensitivities of the spying operations they describe.

Unlike drone attacks, which the administration has begun to acknowledge publicly and provide legal justifications for, cyberattacks are still regarded as part of a secret arsenal that officials will not discuss.

The attacks described in the budget documents appear to be on a far smaller scale than the series of attacks on Iran, which were part of a classified operation called Olympic Games.

The Post reported a parallel effort, code-named GENIE, which it described as an effort by American intelligence officials working for the N.S.A. and the military's Cyber Command to insert surreptitious controls into foreign computer networks. That computer code, a form of malware, allows American officials to hijack the computers or route some of their data to servers that enable American espionage.

It is unclear how many, if any, of those 231 operations were merely for espionage or data manipulation, and how many may have been intended to destroy or disable infrastructure. Computerized espionage is not new, though the sophistication and scale of it has increased in recent years.

Offensive operations intended to alter data, turn off networks or destroy machines — which is what made the Iran operation so complex and unusual — are a far newer phenomenon. President Obama, in an executive order signed last year, has reserved the right to decide when the United States should conduct such operations. It is not clear how many of the 231 he approved.

Diplomatically, the disclosure of the latest Snowden documents poses a new challenge to Mr. Obama. He has pressed China to cease its own cyberoperations in the United States, many of which are aimed at the theft of intellectual property including corporate secrets and the plans for the F-35 Joint Strike Fighter, the country's most expensive new weapons system.

The Chinese have responded that America also conducts extensive cyberoperations, including against China, and will doubtless use the most recent disclosures to press that case. So far, Mr. Obama's effort to get the Chinese engaged in a deeper dialogue on cyberissues has yielded discussions, but little fruit.

The Pentagon has insisted that the United States does not engage in economic espionage, the specialty of Chinese forces like Unit 61398, a People's Liberation Army operation behind many of the intrusions into American systems.

But it does conduct what specialists call "network exploitation," which it distinguishes from "attacks," to obtain military or intelligence secrets and intercept cell and digital communications. Attacks, at least as defined by the military, would involve destruction of computer equipment or the facilities those networks run.

The Post said a budget document defined network exploitation as "surreptitious virtual or physical access to create and sustain a presence inside targeted systems or facilities." That appears to be part of the offensive operations, and can often pave the way to "facilitate future access," the document said.

The documents indicate that the N.S.A. spent $25 million on "covert purchases of software vulnerabilities." These are often flaws in commercial software, often in the near-ubiquitous Windows operating system, that make it possible to secretly enter and manipulate data.

The bulk of the work inside the N.S.A. is conducted by the Tailored Access Operations group, one of the most secretive units in a secretive agency.

Recently, Gen. Keith B. Alexander, who directs the N.S.A. and commands the military's Cyber Command, spoke publicly of creating 40 cyberteams, including 13 focused on offensive operations.

The defensive operations include protections for the American military and other government agencies, and efforts to detect broad cyberattacks launched on the United States.

To Save on Defense, Hire Rivals

OPINION | BY JACQUES S. GANSLER | FEB. 26, 2014

WASHINGTON — Recent proposals to slash the troop levels of the regular Army illustrate how much pressure the United States government is under to shrink its military budget, even as it revamps and re-equips its forces for future conflicts. To meet all of those goals at the same time, we need to turn to one of the commercial world's most basic cost-control weapons — competition.

That means letting more than one company supply a system or service — for example, having two suppliers of jet engines for one type of fighter. Or, perhaps, maintaining contractual relationships with several suppliers so they can compete for the next contract. These strategies contain costs in the long run and spur innovation. In the end, the military gets the best equipment at more affordable prices.

But recently, the Pentagon appears to have been operating on a different principle — that the lowest bid is the defining criterion for awarding contracts. For sure, initial cost is important, especially in today's economy. But making it the most important consideration ends up costing the government and taxpayers more. That's because the government — like any other customer — must balance price against value. And in combat, where performance is critical, value means what a product can do and how dependable it is over time.

Eliminating comparisons of capability and performance has the unintended consequence of discouraging competing bids from companies that offer a more capable product at a price they cannot afford to lower. Later, a sole bidder might be unable to deliver at its lowball price, in which case the company could see its choices as eating the extra cost, cheapening the product, or sticking the government with a higher bill. In the past, the resolution has too often been just charging taxpayers a higher-than-promised price for a product that might still be inferior to what another company could have offered. And there is little incentive for the producer to improve the product.

I first noticed a trend toward considering price alone several years ago, when the Air Force was acquiring new airborne refueling tankers. After two rounds of a bruising fight against the Airbus planes offered by the European Aeronautic Defense and Space Company (now the Airbus Group), Boeing won the $35 billion contract in 2011 by offering a very low price. The aftermath was predictable: higher-than-expected costs, with the total still unclear.

On two more recent contracts — for replacing the president's 40-year-old Marine One aircraft, and for producing the Air Force's Combat Rescue Helicopter — the Pentagon has found itself with a single bidder, a Sikorsky-Lockheed team. Other would-be bidders concluded that the Pentagon's requirements pointed to a smaller, less capable helicopter than the ones they made, which might have cost somewhat more but would have been more useful and more durable.

Competition is a driving force in America's commercial marketplace; we all benefit from it. Some say its rewards are harder to see in the defense industry, where there is one primary American customer — the Pentagon. But history clearly demonstrates that innovation and cost-restraint follow effective competition.

One example was a competition known in the aerospace industry as the "Great Engine War" of the 1980s. Pratt & Whitney had been the sole provider of engines for the Air Force's F-15 and F-16 fighter jets. But when the company's engines began experiencing reliability problems and increasing operating costs, the Air Force opted for a head-to-head competition against Pratt & Whitney's biggest rival, General Electric. In 1984, the Air Force split the multibillion-dollar contract between the two, with G.E. taking 75 percent of the first order.

The result: With both companies simultaneously meeting the continuing demand for more engines, each kept making its products more reliable and capable, even as manufacturing costs fell. Over the next 20 years, the Air Force saved an estimated $3 billion to $4 billion.

This continuous competition model was especially useful in the 1990s, when the Cold War had ended and mergers and acquisitions were shrinking the list of top Pentagon contractors — to eight in 1999 from 36 in 1993. Government officials realized that something had to be done to maintain competition. By splitting production among multiple companies (and awarding the larger share based on a balance between price and previous performance), the services improved long-run cost control and performance in a number of weapons systems, including Tomahawk missiles and Aegis-equipped destroyers.

But the pendulum has now swung back, it seems. In 2011, the Pentagon decided it could not afford to fund an alternative engine for its F-35 Joint Strike Fighter — which, at a potential cost of nearly $400 billion for more than 2,400 fighters, promises to become the largest single weapons program in American history. Rather than keep a team from General Electric and Rolls-Royce involved in the program, it chose to stick with only the engine supplier it already had, Pratt & Whitney, handing that firm a new monopoly.

In December, the Center for Strategic and International Studies reported that by 2012, the share of awards made by the Navy without competition had risen to 54 percent, and by the Air Force to 63 percent.

To be sure, it can be difficult politically to argue for spending more now to reap larger savings and improvements later, especially when the military must stretch its dollars. But history's lesson is clear: Continuous competition, over time, lowers costs, boosts performance and yields technological advancement.

If monopolies are created in a quest for short-term savings, taxpayers eventually pay more and our country is less safe.

JACQUES S. GANSLER, who teaches at the University of Maryland School of Public Policy, was under secretary of defense for acquisition, technology and logistics in the Clinton administration.

A Better, Not Bigger, Military Budget

EDITORIAL | BY THE NEW YORK TIMES | FEB. 29, 2016

GIVEN RECENT HISTORY, the next president can expect to face an even more unpredictable world than the one President Obama is dealing with. Russia, China, Syria, Iran, North Korea, the Islamic State — the list of security challenges is daunting. It will require smart policy choices backed by a powerful military to protect American interests.

So far, the candidates have not sufficiently explained their approaches to military spending which, at $580 billion for 2016, is half of the federal discretionary budget. The toughest talk comes from the Republicans who lean dangerously toward a one-dimensional view of American strength that is over-reliant on an all-powerful military.

"I will make our military so big, powerful and strong that no one will mess with us," Donald Trump says. But what does that mean? This is the guy who extolled the power of nuclear deterrence in a recent debate, but didn't know it relies on three types of forces — missiles, planes and submarines.

Like his rivals for the party's nomination — Senator Marco Rubio, Senator Ted Cruz and Gov. John Kasich — Mr. Trump supports lifting the caps on the defense budget. Some of the candidates act as if these fiscal restraints were imposed by Mr. Obama, when in fact they resulted from a 2011 compromise between the White House and the Republican-led Congress. The caps are overly restrictive, but they have helped rein in out-of-control military spending.

Mr. Rubio wants to "restore military strength" by building more ships and submarines, reversing troop cuts and expanding missile defenses. That would cost an additional $1 trillion over the next 10 years, Benjamin Friedman, a defense expert at the Cato Institute, estimates. Although Mr. Cruz is eager to shrink the rest of the government, his plans to salvage a "shockingly undermanned and ill-prepared" fighting force would increase military spending by $2.5 trillion over

ADAM MAIDA

eight years, Mr. Friedman says. Mr. Kasich would also raise military spending, but more slowly than Mr. Rubio and Mr. Cruz.

Giving the Pentagon a blank check does not ensure security. It got most of what it wanted in the decade after 9/11, yet America still struggles to keep Afghanistan and Iraq from falling to insurgents.

The Republican candidates mislead the public when they say the military is hollowed out; it is the world's most advanced fighting force, with a larger budget than the next seven countries combined. Still, the endless wars have taken a toll on troops and weapons. There is also a budget crisis coming, because many of the new systems under development will reach their peak funding years in the 2020s.

Before any infusion of new funds, the Pentagon, which has wasted billions of dollars on misguided programs, needs to prove it can be a better steward. Congress needs to reform the military health care program, whose costs are spiraling out of control. One place to save: Scale back the planned $1 trillion, 30-year modernization of a nuclear arsenal that will never be used and spend the money on conventional weapons that are needed to fight the Islamic State and other threats. Hillary Clinton and Senator Bernie Sanders, unlike the Republican candidates, have said they are open to this.

Mrs. Clinton has advocated the idea of "smart power," which relies on a range of tools, diplomatic as well as military, to keep the nation safe. She has said she would name a commission to study military spending. Mr. Sanders wants a "robust military" but opposes spending increases.

America needs a strong and technologically advanced military, but politically driven excessive investment in the Pentagon has too often meant short shrift for the State Department and its diplomatic missions, as well as cuts in domestic programs that hurt the most vulnerable citizens. It is crucial for the next president to get that balance right.

A Better, Not Fatter, Defense Budget

EDITORIAL | BY THE NEW YORK TIMES | MAY 9, 2016

TO HEAR SOME military commanders and members of Congress talk, the American military is worn out and in desperate need of more money. After more than a decade in Iraq and Afghanistan, they say, troops are lagging in training and new weaponry, which is jeopardizing their ability to defeat the Islamic State and deal with potential conflicts with Russia and China.

While increased funding for some programs may be needed, total military spending, at nearly $600 billion annually, is not too low. The trouble is, the investment has often yielded poor results, with the Pentagon, Congress and the White House all making bad judgments, playing budget games and falling under the sway of defense industry lobbyists. Current military spending is 50 percent higher in real terms than it was before 9/11, yet the number of active duty and reserve troops is 6 percent smaller.

For nearly a decade after 9/11, the Pentagon had a virtual blank check; the base defense budget rose, in adjusted dollars, from $378 billion in 1998 to $600 billion in 2010. As the military fought Al Qaeda and the Taliban, billions of dollars were squandered on unnecessary items, including new weapons that ran late and over budget like the troubled F-35 jet fighter.

The waste and the budget games continue with the House Armed Services Committee approving a $583 billion total defense authorization bill for 2017 last month that skirts the across-the-board caps imposed by Congress in 2011 on discretionary federal spending.

The caps are supposed to restrain domestic and military spending equally, but defense hawks have insisted on throwing more money at the Pentagon. That doesn't encourage efficiency or wise choices. The panel took $18 billion from a $59 billion off-budget account, which has become a slush fund renewed annually to finance the wars in Iraq,

Afghanistan and other trouble spots, and is not subject to the budget caps, and repurposed that money for use in the $524 billion base military budget.

The move will underwrite the purchase of more ships, jet fighters, helicopters and other big-ticket weapons that the Pentagon didn't request and will keep the Army from falling below 480,000 active-duty troops. It also means the war account will run out of money next April. Representative Mac Thornberry, the Republican chairman of the committee, apparently assumes the next president will be forced to ask for, and Congress will be forced to approve, more money for the war account. This sleight of hand runs the risk that troops overseas, at some point, could be deprived of some resources, at least temporarily. The full House should reject this maneuver.

Many defense experts, liberals and centrists as well as hawks, agree that more investment is needed in maintenance, training and modernizing aging weapons and equipment. These needs were identified years ago, yet the Pentagon and Congress have chosen to invest in excessively costly high-tech weaponry while deferring maintenance and other operational expenses.

The Pentagon can do with far fewer than the 1,700 F-35s it plans on buying. It should pare back on President Obama's $1 trillion plan to replace nearly every missile, submarine, aircraft and warhead in the nuclear arsenal. Defense officials recently reported that 22 percent of all military bases will not be needed by 2019. Civilian positions will have to be reduced, while reforms in health care and the military procurement system need to be carried out. All of these changes make good sense, given the savings they would bring. But they are politically unpalatable; base closings, for instance, have been stubbornly resisted in recent years by lawmakers fearful of angering voters by eliminating jobs in communities that are economically dependent on those bases.

Todd Harrison, a defense budget expert with the Center for Strategic and International Studies, says that sustaining the current military force of roughly two million and paying for all the new weapons systems will cost billions more than Congress has allowed under the budget caps. To maintain sensible troop levels, Congress and the administration need to begin honestly addressing the hard fiscal choices that they have largely been loath to make.

Critics Assail Cuts in Foreign Spending as Trump Moves to Boost Military

BY HELENE COOPER AND PETER BAKER | FEB. 27, 2017

WASHINGTON — President Trump's proposal to add $54 billion to the Pentagon budget next year sounds huge at first — a 10 percent increase for a department that already receives more of taxpayers' money than any other part of government.

But the outgoing Obama administration had forecast a $35 billion increase for the Defense Department in fiscal year 2018, so Mr. Trump's share of the proposed increase over and above that figure is $19 billion, according to budget analysts.

Even so, the proposed Pentagon increase has been greeted with criticism from military spending hawks, in part because White House officials say Mr. Trump will call for a significant cut in foreign aid, including programs that military officials say contribute to global stability and are seen as important in helping avoid future conflicts.

Senior administration officials acknowledged on Monday that there were few specifics attached to the bigger budget number proposed for the Pentagon — so it is not yet possible to assess how many more troops, warships or jet-fighters the Pentagon will be able to field with the $54 billion.

"Where we're at in this process is that the number's going to the D.O.D. today, and over the course of the next 10 days to two weeks, we'll be coming up with those types of details," Mick Mulvaney, the president's budget director, said when pressed on plans for Department of Defense spending.

Broadly speaking, Mr. Trump has said his military priorities include buying more warships and warplanes, increasing the number of American ground troops and modernizing the nuclear arsenal. Even so, he will face difficulty in getting such a proposal through Congress, where the threat of mandatory spending cuts known as sequestration has acted as a brake on military spending.

"This is a symbolic gesture," said Todd Harrison, the director of defense budget analysis at the Center for Strategic and International Studies. "What Trump is proposing is increasing defense spending and paying for it by cutting nondefense spending. There's no way Democrats are going to go for that."

Under sequestration rules, Republicans would need Democrats to increase the military budget, a requirement that is likely to stymie Republican efforts to pay for increases in the Pentagon budget with cuts in other spending, including social programs.

At the Defense Department, where military leaders always welcome more money, officials were muted about Mr. Trump's budget proposal. What is more, Mr. Trump joined his call for increased military spending with a critique of the military, implying that the nation's armed forces need more money because they have failed at winning wars.

"We have to start winning wars again," Mr. Trump said. "I have to say, when I was young, in high school and college, everybody used to say we never lost a war. We never lost a war, remember?"

He continued: "And now we never win a war. We never win. And don't fight to win. We don't fight to win. We've either got to win or don't fight at all."

Mr. Trump was born in 1946, the year after World War II ended. The only wars fought when he was young were not American victories — he was 7 when the Korean War ended in a stalemate, and he was in college when American forces were bogged down in Vietnam. When he was in his 40s and 50s, the United States conducted a successful military operation in Panama, reversed Iraq's invasion and occupation of Kuwait, and drove Serbian forces out of Kosovo.

But Mr. Trump was channeling public exhaustion after more than 15 years of warfare since the Sept. 11, 2001, attacks, including the still unresolved conflicts in Afghanistan and Iraq.

Mick Mulvaney, the president's budget director, spoke on Monday about the budget proposal.

Mr. Trump gave no indication of how he would have ensured victory in either of those places or what he planned to do. Defense Secretary Jim Mattis briefed the president's team on Monday on potential strategies for defeating the Islamic State, which has operated in Iraq and Syria.

Still, even the wars believed to be outright American victories by the public are not necessarily so, according to Andrew Exum, a retired Army Ranger and a Defense Department official in the Obama administration.

"Those victories were not as decisive as we remember: It took another 100 years, after the civil rights acts of the 1960s, before the North truly won the Civil War, while the peace that ended the First World War begat the Second World War, and the peace that ended the Second World War begat the Cold War and its many constituent conflicts," Mr. Exum said. "What Trump is saying resonates because it's based more on the myths we tell ourselves than the histories written down in long, dense books."

Former and current American military officials agreed.

"The wars today don't deliver battlefield victories along the lines of what we saw in World War II, with the surrender on the deck of the battleship Missouri," said David W. Barno, a retired Army lieutenant general and former commander of American forces in Afghanistan. "We're fighting enemies with no navies, no air forces or even conventional armies in some cases. Applying only conventional armed forces to these conflicts is not always going to be adequate."

Several former Pentagon officials, including a number of retired generals and admirals, cautioned against cutting the State Department and foreign aid budgets to help pay for increases in Pentagon spending. In a letter to top congressional leaders, the retired military officers wrote that "elevating and strengthening diplomacy and development alongside defense are critical to keeping America safe."

"We know from our service in uniform that many of the crises our nation faces do not have military solutions alone," the generals and admirals wrote. "The military will lead the fight against terrorism on the battlefield, but it needs strong civilian partners in the battle against the drivers of extremism — lack of opportunity, insecurity, injustice and hopelessness."

James G. Stavridis, a retired admiral who signed the letter, said on Monday that most senior military leaders believed it was unwise to cut development aid and diplomacy funding.

"So often, the far less expensive 'soft power' tools — humanitarian relief, medical diplomacy, foreign aid, strategic communications — are under sister agencies such as state and A.I.D.," said Mr. Stavridis, a former NATO commander who now serves as the dean of the Fletcher School of Law and Diplomacy at Tufts University, referring to the State Department and the Agency for International Development. "Cutting them harshly would be a mistake."

Even Mr. Mattis expressed those views before being named defense secretary. "If you don't fully fund the State Department, then I need to buy more ammunition," he said during congressional testimony in 2013, when he was head of the military's Central Command.

Senator John McCain, Republican of Arizona and the chairman of the Armed Services Committee, recently released a report calling for an increase in military spending to $640 billion in the next fiscal year, not the $603 billion that Mr. Trump proposed.

In a statement on Monday, Mr. McCain said Mr. Trump's proposal was insufficient. "With a world on fire, America cannot secure peace through strength with just 3 percent more than President Obama's budget," Mr. McCain said. "We can and must do better."

After the Pentagon budget number was released on Monday, the stocks of the largest military contractors rose 1 percent to 2 percent during trading. Lockheed Martin, Boeing, General Dynamics and Northrop Grumman, which pay relatively high dividends, had already seen their stocks rise to record levels in a rally that began last summer.

Investors will now want to see how any budget increases would be divided among weapons programs to determine which companies would benefit the most.

CHRISTOPHER DREW contributed reporting from New York.

Will There Be a Ban on Killer Robots?

BY ADAM SATARIANO | OCT. 19, 2018

LONDON — An autonomous missile under development by the Pentagon uses software to choose between targets. An artificially intelligent drone from the British military identifies firing points on its own. Russia showcases tanks that don't need soldiers inside for combat.

A.I. technology has for years led military leaders to ponder a future of warfare that needs little human involvement. But as capabilities have advanced, the idea of autonomous weapons reaching the battlefield is becoming less hypothetical.

The possibility of software and algorithms making life-or-death decisions has added new urgency to efforts by a group called the Campaign To Stop Killer Robots that has pulled together arms control advocates, humans rights groups and technologists to urge the United Nations to craft a global treaty that bans weapons without people at the controls. Like cyberspace, where there aren't clear rules of engagement for online attacks, no red lines have been defined over the use of automated weaponry.

Without a nonproliferation agreement, some diplomats fear the world will plunge into an algorithm-driven arms race.

In a speech at the start of the United Nations General Assembly in New York on Sept. 25, Secretary General António Guterres listed the technology as a global risk alongside climate change and growing income inequality.

"Let's call it as it is: The prospect of machines with the discretion and power to take human life is morally repugnant," Mr. Guterres said.

Two weeks earlier, Federica Mogherini, the European Union's high representative for foreign affairs and security policy, said the weapons "impact our collective security," and that decisions of life and death must remain in human hands.

Twenty-six countries have called for an explicit ban that requires some form of human control in the use of force. But the prospects for an A.I. weapons ban are low. Several influential countries including the United States are unwilling to place limits while the technology is still in development.

Diplomats have been unable to reach a consensus about how a global policy can be implemented or enforced. Some have called for a voluntary agreement, others want rules that are legally binding.

A meeting of more than 70 countries organized by the United Nations in Geneva in August made little headway, as the United States and others said a better understanding of the technology was needed before sweeping restrictions can be made. Another round of talks are expected to be held later this year.

Some have raised concerns that a ban will affect civilian research. Much of the most cutting-edge work in artificial intelligence and machine learning is from universities and companies such as Google and Facebook. But much of that technology can be adapted to military use.

"A lot of A.I. technologies are being developed outside of government and released to the public," said Jack Clark, a spokesman for OpenAI, a Silicon Valley group that advocates for more measured adoption of artificial intelligence. "These technologies have generic capabilities that can be applied in many different domains, including in weaponization."

Major technical challenges remain before any robot weaponry reaches the battlefield. Maaike Verbruggen, a researcher at the Institute for European Studies who specializes in emerging military and security technology, said communication is still limited, making it hard for humans to understand why artificially intelligent machines make decisions. Better safeguards also are needed to ensure robots act as predicted, she said.

But significant advancements will come in the next two decades, said Derrick Maple, an analyst who studies military spending for the market research firm Jane's by IHS Markit in London. As the technology changes, he said, any international agreement could be futile; countries will tear it apart in the event of war.

"You cannot dictate the rules of engagement," Mr. Maple said. "If the enemy is going to do something, then you have to do something as well. No matter what rules you put in place, in a conflict situation the rules will go out the window."

Defense contractors, identifying a new source of revenue, are eager to build the next-generation machinery. Last year, Boeing reorganized its defense business to include a division focused on drones and other unmanned weaponry. The company also bought Aurora Flight Sciences, a maker of autonomous aircrafts. Other defense contractors such as Lockheed Martin, BAE Systems and Raytheon are making similar shifts.

Mr. Maple, who has worked in the field for over four decades, estimates military spending on unmanned military vehicles such as drones and ships will top $120 billion over the next decade.

No completely autonomous weapons are known to be currently deployed on the battlefield, but militaries have been using technology to automate for years. Israel's Iron Dome air-defense system automatically detects and destroys incoming rockets. South Korea uses autonomous equipment to detect movements along the North Korean border.

Mr. Maple expects more collaboration between humans and machines before there is an outright transfer of responsibility to robots. Researchers, for example, are studying how aircrafts and tanks can be backed by artificially intelligent fleets of drones.

In 2016, the Pentagon highlighted its capabilities during a test in the Mojave Desert. More than 100 drones were dropped from a fighter jet in a disorganized heap, before quickly coming together to race toward and encircle a target. From a radar video shared by the Pentagon, the drones look like a flock of migrating starlings.

There were no humans at the controls of the drones as they flew overhead, and the machines didn't look much different from those any person can buy from a consumer-electronics store. The drones were programmed to communicate with each other independently to collectively organize and reach the target.

"They are a collective organism, sharing one distributed brain for decision-making and adapting to each other like swarms in nature," William Roper, director of the Pentagon's strategic capabilities office, said at the time.

To those fearful of the advancement of autonomous weapons, the implications were clear.

"You're delegating the decision to kill to a machine," said Thomas Hajnoczi, the head of disarmament department for the Austrian government. "A machine doesn't have any measure of moral judgment or mercy."

CHAPTER 5

Case Study: The F-35 Joint Strike Fighter

With all its stealth and advanced technological capabilities, the F-35 Joint Strike Fighter — so called because it would be adapted by various branches of the military to meet different attack requirements — may simply be remembered as one of the most expensive weapons development projects ever. Focusing on the F-35 project, with its delays and the various investments that went into its completion, serves as an opportunity to see the military-industrial complex spending apparatus in action.

Painting a Rosy Picture of a Costly Fighter Jet

BY LESLIE WAYNE | JUNE 22, 2007

LE BOURGET, FRANCE, JUNE 21 — With jets screaming overhead, macho often mixes with Mach 1 here at the Paris air show. But the Lockheed Martin Corporation chose a softer approach to show the might of its next-generation radar-evading, supersonic fighter jet.

It commissioned nine international artists to portray the multibillion-dollar combat plane in a variety of imaginary scenes — sailing over the Canadian Northwest, hovering over a British naval carrier and gliding above Sydney Harbor in Australia.

The unveiling of the paintings here was a case of making virtue out

Lockheed Martin unveiled paintings of the F-35 Lightning II at the Paris air show. The Joint Strike Fighter program, a coalition of nine countries, has invested billions of dollars to design, finance and build the jet.

of necessity. Lockheed's Joint Strike Fighter program — the largest program in Pentagon aviation with an eventual price tag exceeding $600 billion — is only now moving off the drawing board and into first flight.

Only one Joint Strike Fighter, also called the F-35 Lightning II, has been produced so far, to be used in testing, with 13 more planes scheduled for next year. Lockheed continues to push ahead amid concerns over the program's costs, its ambitious development schedule and an international political drama as Lockheed and the eight other partner nations in the project continue to bump elbows, and sometimes heads.

The Joint Strike Fighter program is unique in military aviation. With this program, the Pentagon rewrote the rules on how fighter jets are made. It put together an international coalition to design, finance and build the jet jointly rather than having a single country, typically the United States, build the jet and sell it to others. This required the countries to share sensitive technologies, invest large sums of money and act in the best interest of the group, not their own nation.

The sums of money involved are staggering, and growing. The Pentagon has estimated the program's development and procurement costs at $276 billion, with an additional $347 billion needed to operate and support the planes in the field. Already, the program is $31.6 billion over budget, slightly behind schedule and facing daunting technical challenges.

Yet Brig. Gen. Charles R. Davis of the Air Force, the program's executive director, was optimistic about the program's recent accomplishments — not the least of which was keeping all nine nations on board.

"We're well on our way," General Davis said at a Lockheed news conference. "And we will grow."

Others say there is reason for optimism. Alexandra Ashbourne of Ashbourne Strategic Consulting in London, which specializes in military contractors, said, "The program is looking rosier than it has been in a while.

"It had been running late," Ms. Ashbourne said. "And there were a number of other issues involving technology transfers. But these concerns seem to have been allayed in the last few months. A lot of people are beginning to feel that this is a most amazing craft."

From a pilot's perspective, the F-35 Lightning is a dream machine. It is intended to replace the F-16 and other fighter jets of that generation, which total around 4,000 worldwide. The F-35's stealth technology makes it invisible to radar. It flies faster than the speed of sound and is filled with the latest aviation electronics.

At the air show, a life-size mock-up of the plane attracted a crowd of military aviators, who climbed into the single-seat, single-engine airplane as though it were real. Jon Beesley, chief test pilot for the F-35, stood by in his blue flight suit, eagerly explaining the plane's technical details to this knowledgeable crowd.

Yet for all its sizzle, the F-35 is designed to be affordable — a sort of Chevrolet of the skies — so that the nations in the partnership, and

Visitors at the Paris air show climb aboard a mock-up of the single-seat, single-engine F-35. Only one has been produced so far, and 13 more are expected next year.

ones that are not, can add it to their fleets. The terms of the international partnership mean that Lockheed must look around the world for the best technologies and the most efficient production processes for the craft.

But the program's ambitious schedule and technological challenges are raising concerns, especially at the Government Accountability Office, which oversees the program.

The G.A.O. called the decision by Lockheed and the Air Force to begin to produce the craft in low numbers before all the testing has been done a "high-risk strategy." Overlapping the testing with early production could easily backfire and result in delays and cost overruns should modifications in the design or the manufacturing of the plane be required, the G.A.O. said in a report issued last March entitled "Joint Strike Fighter: Progress Made and Challenges Remain."

As a result, the G.A.O. recommended slowing the program until the design was further refined.

Tom Burbage, Lockheed's F-35 program manager, could not disagree more. He argues that technological advances allow the company to telescope the development and manufacturing processes and that this approach will reduce risk of delays and cost overruns.

"I do not agree it adds extra risk," Mr. Burbage said of Lockheed's approach, speaking at the news conference. "We are doing it the right way, and what the G.A.O. says will do just the opposite."

Adding to the complication is that the international consortium plans to produce three variations of the plane — one that will land at regular air fields, one to land on carriers and a third, championed by the Marines and the British, that will have a vertical takeoff and landing.

The Pentagon has said it wants to buy 2,458 F-35s, which will be divided among the services, with the Air Force taking the bulk, 1,763. Deliveries are expected to begin in 2010. The other international partners have indicated they will buy 600 to 700. And as they are built, planes will be made available for sale to nations not in the program. The jets will cost around $75 million each for the basic version and up to $90 million for more advanced designs.

But a quarrel has broken out between the Navy and Marines over the vertical version. Internal Navy memos that were obtained by DefenseNews, a trade publication, indicate that the Navy, which oversees the Marine budget, would like to see the Marine version dropped from the program. It is the most expensive F-35, and the most technically complicated.

"The Marines want a fighter that can land anywhere," said Loren Thompson, a military analyst at the Lexington Institute, a research group based in Arlington, Va. "But the admirals don't like what the Marines are asking for."

The Marines, though, have a powerful ally in Britain, which wants to buy 138 vertical-lift F-35s as a replacement for the Harrier, which can also take off and land vertically. And analysts say that it would be hard to drop the version of the plane that is so important to Britain.

The international partners — Britain, Italy, the Netherlands, Norway, Turkey, Canada, Australia and Denmark — have invested around $4 billion in the F-35. In return, they are given part of the design and the production, based on their skills and cost structure. Final assembly will be done in the United States, although negotiations are under way for a possible second assembly site in northern Italy.

The G.A.O. has also warned that the enormity of the program coupled with a large budget deficit in the United States may lead to cutbacks.

But General Davis, the Pentagon official overseeing the program day to day, has more immediate worries.

"My biggest challenge," he said, "is just to keep it on schedule."

Audit of Pentagon Spending Finds $70 Billion in Waste

BY CHRISTOPHER DREW | MARCH 29, 2011

DESPITE IMPROVEMENTS, more than half of the Pentagon's big weapons systems still cost more than they should, with management failures adding at least $70 billion to the projected costs over the last two years, government auditors said Tuesday.

The Government Accountability Office, a Congressional watchdog, said the biggest program, the F-35 Joint Strike Fighter, accounted for $28 billion of that increase. Other systems also had significant cost overruns, the agency said, adding that the increases could force the Pentagon to cut the number of ships and planes it buys.

The auditors said many of the problems occurred because the Pentagon began building the systems before the designs were fully tested.

The findings were significant because Congress and the Obama administration have promised to change many of the practices that have long allowed weapons costs to spiral out of control.

President Obama signed a law in 2009 to improve contracting. The accountability office said that Pentagon officials had done a better job in starting new programs. But the agency also found that most of the new programs were not "fully adhering" to the best procedures, leaving them "at a higher risk for cost growth and schedule delays."

Pentagon officials questioned some of the calculations. But Nancy L. Spruill, a Pentagon acquisition official, added in a letter to the auditors that the military was determined to "address cost growth where it is real and unacceptable."

The defense secretary, Robert M. Gates, has acknowledged that the Pentagon lacked discipline as its budget more than doubled after the 9/11 terrorist attacks. But with military budgets tightening, Mr. Gates has canceled several expensive systems and sought simpler alternatives.

All told, the accountability office said, the projected cost of the Pentagon's largest programs has risen by $135 billion, or 9 percent, to $1.68 trillion since 2008.

It estimated that about $65 billion of that increase resulted from decisions to buy more of some systems, like mine-resistant vehicles and Navy destroyers, than had been planned.

But it said the other $70 billion of increases appeared "to be indicative of production problems and inefficiencies or flawed initial cost estimates."

The auditors also found that a significant part of the total cost increase for nearly 100 programs came from just a few of the largest and oldest ones.

The F-35, which is supposed to become the main fighter for the Air Force, the Navy and the Marines, had by far the worst problems. The Pentagon has revamped the program, led by Lockheed Martin, twice over the last year. It has budgeted an additional $6 billion for development, as well as the projected $28 billion increase in production costs, for a program that is expected to cost well over $300 billion.

The report indicated that the Pentagon also had to spend $9 billion more on research and development to fix problems with satellites and other systems that had already entered production.

The auditors said the biggest problems occurred when the Pentagon changed the capabilities it sought or started production before critical technologies were ready.

Defense Chief Ends Probation Status of Marine Warplane

BY THOM SHANKER | JAN. 20, 2012

NAVAL AIR STATION PATUXENT RIVER, MD. — Defense Secretary Leon E. Panetta visited a flight testing center along the shores of Chesapeake Bay on Friday to give a lift to the beleaguered F-35 Joint Strike Fighter, announcing that he was taking the Marine Corps version of the costly warplane off probation.

Mr. Panetta's decision to embrace the F-35, one of the most expensive weapons efforts in history, comes as the Defense Department has been ordered to cut at least $485 billion from its budget over the next decade.

"We need to make sure we are on the cutting edge," Mr. Panetta said in describing his personal support, and that of the Pentagon, for next-generation war-fighting technology, including the F-35 jet fighter program.

Mr. Panetta said that the F-35 was "absolutely vital to maintaining our air superiority," but cautioned that it was important "to get this right."

He said there had been enough progress in fixing technical problems that he could reverse the decision by his predecessor, Robert M. Gates, to put the plane on a probationary testing status.

The Marine Corps version is especially complex because it is designed to take off from the shortest of runways, such as a rough strip of land or the deck of a smaller warship, and to land vertically, like a helicopter.

Designing a stealthy, advanced fighter that can perform those feats has been daunting and costly. The F-35's estimated overall cost is $382 billion for up to 2,456 planes. The radar-evading aircraft will also have versions for the Air Force and the Navy.

Shortly after Mr. Panetta's announcement, Gen. James F. Amos, the Marine Corps commandant, released a statement praising the decision.

"I welcome the secretary of defense's announcement removing the F-35B Lightning II from 'probation' and granting it full status commensurate with the other two variants of the Joint Strike Fighter," General Amos said. "I continue to be encouraged by the strong and steady progress that the F-35B team has made over the past year."

When Mr. Gates announced the plane's probation last year, he said the program should be canceled if it did not show progress within two years.

Among the serious problems that led to Mr. Gates's decision were insufficient intake of air via a duct to the engine and an unacceptable wobbling when the jet hovered over a landing spot.

Mr. Panetta's decision to lift the probation on the Marine Corps version reflected an assessment of progress — but also the importance to the Marine Corps of coming up with a replacement for its Harrier jump-jet, which has proved its value in countering insurgencies and terrorists in rugged, remote areas. The Marine Corps' F-35 version would be the only American jet fighter to replicate the aging Harrier's capability for short takeoff and vertical landing.

Even so, Pentagon officials and industry analysts expect that when Mr. Panetta releases the Defense Department's official budget proposals, he will call for postponing the purchase of a large number of the F-35s sought by the various branches.

That option would allow the factories to stay open — protecting jobs — while giving the prime manufacturer, the Lockheed Martin Corporation, more time to work out problems with the jet.

Just as important, it would allow the military to delay tens of billions of dollars in spending at a time when Mr. Panetta must come up with plans to cut about $485 billion from the Pentagon budget over the next decade.

On Friday, Mr. Panetta spoke in a hangar where a Navy version of the F-35 was on display at one end, while at the other was the Marine

Corps variant — its troubled engine intake door yawning wide open for display.

The latest F-35 flight test — seeking to correct a problem in the air intake door was successfully completed last week.

Capt. Erik Etz of the Navy, who serves as director of testing and evaluation for the Navy variants of the F-35, said the program had shown improved rates of actual testing time and, over all, had tallied more than 2,300 hours during more than 1,400 flights.

Work continues on fixing the tail-hook system on the Navy variant, which must take off and land on carriers, as well as solving troubles with the helmet and the night-vision system.

Two Very Troubled Fighter Jets

EDITORIAL | BY THE NEW YORK TIMES | JULY 14, 2012

ECONOMIC PRESSURES ARE forcing justifiable cuts in military spending. The budget control act passed by Congress in 2011 mandated $480 billion in cuts over 10 years, with the possibility of $500 billion more in reductions, beginning next January. After a decade of unrestrained military spending, the Pentagon needs this rebalancing.

With such cuts looming, it is more important than ever to ensure that every defense dollar is spent wisely. Yet problems with two major weapons show how far the Pentagon is from that goal and how dysfunctional its procurement system remains.

The F-35 Joint Strike Fighter was supposed to prove that the Pentagon could build a technologically advanced weapon system within an affordable budget, without huge delays. After the aircraft turned into the Pentagon's biggest budget buster, and performed disappointingly, the Obama administration tried to correct course in 2010. A new report last month by the Government Accountability Office showed that the problems had not been solved.

The Air Force, the Navy and the Marines plan to buy more than 2,400 F-35s through 2037. The accountability office now estimates the total cost of acquisition at nearly $400 billion, up 42 percent from the estimate in 2007; the price per plane has doubled since project development began in 2001. Cost overruns now total $1 billion.

The agency reported other problems as well. It said that the plane would not be in full production until 2019, a delay of six years, and that the small number of planes produced so far were being delivered, on average, one year late. The F-35's overall performance in 2011 was described as "mixed." There also have been difficulties integrating 24 million lines of software code into the complex computer system.

Meanwhile, the F-22 Raptor, the world's costliest and most advanced stealth fighter jet, is also mired in performance problems.

Over the past 18 months, there have been repeated cases in which pilots have suffered dizziness and disorientation from lack of oxygen in the planes, which cost $400 million each.

The Air Force has acknowledged 36 incidents, with 21 of those described as unexplained; three more episodes were reported in recent weeks. For more than a year, Air Force officials have struggled to find a cause of the problem, and last month said they believed that a pressure vest was restricting pilots' breathing and that narrow oxygen hoses were leaking or not delivering enough air. But two pilots who experienced recent hypoxia symptoms were not wearing vests.

Late last year, the Air Force stopped flying the F-22 for five months. Flights have since resumed, but are limited to within 30 minutes of a landing field.

The administration committed early on to reform the acquisition system and rein in escalating costs, but clearly its efforts are not sufficient. Congress and defense contractors have a stake in this too. Many are complaining about the financial and strategic pressures that are forcing defense reductions. They need to worry as much about the billions being wasted.

Costliest Jet, Years in Making, Sees the Enemy: Budget Cuts

BY CHRISTOPHER DREW | NOV. 28, 2012

LEXINGTON PARK, MD. — The Marine version of the F-35 Joint Strike Fighter, already more than a decade in the making, was facing a crucial question: Could the jet, which can soar well past the speed of sound, land at sea like a helicopter?

On an October day last year, with Lt. Col. Fred Schenk at the controls, the plane glided toward a ship off the Atlantic coast and then, its engine rotating straight down, descended gently to the deck at seven feet a second.

There were cheers from the ship's crew members, who "were all shaking my hands and smiling," Colonel Schenk recalled.

The smooth landing helped save that model and breathed new life into the huge F-35 program, the most expensive weapons system in military history. But while Pentagon officials now say that the program is making progress, it begins its 12th year in development years behind schedule, troubled with technological flaws and facing concerns about its relatively short flight range as possible threats grow from Asia.

With a record price tag — potentially in the hundreds of billions of dollars — the jet is likely to become a target for budget cutters. Reining in military spending is on the table as President Obama and Republican leaders in Congress look for ways to avert a fiscal crisis. But no matter what kind of deal is reached in the next few weeks, military analysts expect the Pentagon budget to decline in the next decade as the war in Afghanistan ends and the military is required to do its part to reduce the federal debt.

Behind the scenes, the Pentagon and the F-35's main contractor, Lockheed Martin, are engaged in a conflict of their own over the costs. The relationship "is the worst I've ever seen, and I've been in some

Vice Adm. David Venlet was named to lead the Joint Strike Fighter program in 2010 after problems had left it behind schedule and over budget.

bad ones," Maj. Gen. Christopher Bogdan of the Air Force, a top program official, said in September. "I guarantee you: we will not succeed on this if we do not get past that."

In a battle that is being fought on other military programs as well, the Pentagon has been pushing Lockheed to cut costs much faster while the company is fighting to hold onto a profit. "Lockheed has seemed to be focused on short-term business goals," Frank Kendall, the Pentagon's top weapons buyer, said this month. "And we'd like to see them focus more on execution of the program and successful delivery of the product."

The F-35 was conceived as the Pentagon's silver bullet in the sky — a state-of-the art aircraft that could be adapted to three branches of the military, with advances that would easily overcome the defenses of most foes. The radar-evading jets would not only dodge sophisticated antiaircraft missiles, but they would also give pilots a better picture of enemy threats while enabling allies, who want the planes, too, to fight more closely with American forces.

But the ambitious aircraft instead illustrates how the Pentagon can let huge and complex programs veer out of control and then have a hard time reining them in. The program nearly doubled in cost as Lockheed and the military's own bureaucracy failed to deliver on the most basic promise of a three-in-one jet that would save taxpayers money and be served up speedily.

Lockheed has delivered 41 planes so far for testing and initial training, and Pentagon leaders are slowing purchases of the F-35 to fix the latest technical problems and reduce the immediate costs. A helmet for pilots that projects targeting data onto its visor is too jittery to count on. The tail-hook on the Navy jet has had trouble catching the arresting cable, meaning that version cannot yet land on carriers. And writing and testing the millions of lines of software needed by the jets is so daunting that General Bogdan said, "It scares the heck out of me."

With all the delays — full production is not expected until 2019 — the military has spent billions to extend the lives of older fighters and buy more of them to fill the gap. At the same time, the cost to build each F-35 has risen to an average of $137 million from $69 million in 2001.

The jets would cost taxpayers $396 billion, including research and development, if the Pentagon sticks to its plan to build 2,443 by the late 2030s. That would be nearly four times as much as any other weapons system and two-thirds of the $589 billion the United States has spent on the war in Afghanistan. The military is also desperately trying to figure out how to reduce the long-term costs of operating the planes, now projected at $1.1 trillion.

"The plane is unaffordable," said Winslow T. Wheeler, an analyst at the Project on Government Oversight, a nonprofit group in Washington.

Todd Harrison, an analyst at the Center for Strategic and Budgetary Assessments, a research group in Washington, said Pentagon officials had little choice but to push ahead, especially after already spending $65 billion on the fighter. "It is simultaneously too big to fail and too big to succeed," he said. "The bottom line here is that they've crammed too much into the program. They were asking one fighter to do three different jobs, and they basically ended up with three different fighters."

While weapons cost overruns have long been a problem, the F-35 is also running into the changing budget realities, and a new focus on rivalry with China, that will probably require shifting money to a broader mix of planes.

Yet, for years, the problems with the F-35 raised few red flags, as money flowed freely after the 2001 terror attacks and enthusiasm for a three-in-one jet blinded officials in the Clinton and Bush administrations and in Congress to its overly ambitious design. Now, unless the Pentagon can substantially reduce the price of each plane, analysts say, it may be lucky to buy 1,200 to 1,800.

Robert J. Stevens, the chief executive of Lockheed Martin, said company officials were "working as aggressively as we can" to fix the problems and cut costs. Vice Adm. David Venlet, who now runs the program at the Pentagon, said he was confident that "good old-fashioned engineering is going to lick" the flaws. But he declined to predict how many planes would be bought.

"It's a very fair conversation that ought to be had for the country," he said.

'ACQUISITION MALPRACTICE'

Right from the start, Pentagon officials were warned of the dangers of beginning to produce an aircraft before it was tested. And right from the start, Pentagon officials did not listen.

The roots of the problems go back to the mid-1990s, when military officials pitched the F-35 as simple and affordable, like a Chevrolet of the skies, with the three versions sharing 70 to 80 percent of their parts. The planes would also be versatile, capable of fighting other planes but focused mainly on attacking ground targets.

An F-35B, the Marine Corps version of the Joint Strike Fighter.

Pentagon officials thought advances in computer modeling would simulate so precisely the way the F-35 would fly that only minor problems would be discovered in the flight tests.

And given a ban on exporting the F-22, the top stealth fighter, moving quickly on the F-35 would lock up foreign buyers and keep Europe from creating its own stealth planes.

"There was this big desire to kill the competition," said Richard L. Aboulafia, an analyst at the Teal Group in Fairfax, Va.

Lockheed beat out Boeing for the F-35 contract in October 2001.

Pentagon testing experts and Congressional auditors warned as the program got under way that it would be wiser to "fly before you buy." They cautioned that some of the new technologies were not ready and that years of flight tests would find flaws that the simulations had not anticipated.

Lockheed and the joint Air Force and Navy office that runs the program countered that the sooner they started building a sizable number of planes, the sooner they could realize economies of scale that would lower the price of each plane, even if some needed updating.

But almost immediately, the project proved to be incredibly complicated. Lockheed's initial designs were late and had to be redone, delaying the manufacture of parts for the test models. While most military programs start building before all the testing is done, the Pentagon took that to an extreme, starting production of the F-35s in 2007, before flight tests had even begun.

Mr. Kendall, who became the Pentagon's top weapons buyer in May, has said that diving into production so soon amounted to "acquisition malpractice."

Mr. Harrison, the analyst at the budget center, said the willingness to "roll the dice" reflected the peculiar incentives at the Pentagon, where rushing into production creates jobs and locks in political support, even if it allows programs to drift into trouble. Lockheed and its suppliers on the F-35 employ 35,000 workers, with some in nearly every Congressional district.

"The military services want to get the planes as quickly as possible," Mr. Harrison said. "The defense industry wants to start producing as quickly as possible. But it's not in the best interest of taxpayers, and it ends up catching up with you."

Asked who protects the taxpayer, he said, "That's what the Pentagon's civilian leadership is supposed to bring."

But with the Iraq and Afghanistan wars raging, Robert M. Gates, who was then the defense secretary, did not deal with the problems with the F-35 until late 2009 and early 2010, when he fired the general in charge and brought in Admiral Venlet, a former fighter pilot who had overseen testing of Navy aircraft. According to the admiral, Mr. Gates said, "Dave, the program has made small adjustments over the years and persistently disappointed people."

Then, sweeping his finger in a wide arc, Mr. Gates added, "If you evaluate that we need a big adjustment, tell me, and I'll make it, so we don't disappoint any more."

CONTRACTOR IN THE HOT SEAT

Admiral Venlet's first move was to bring in technical experts from the services who had been shut out of the program. He said his predecessors had given Lockheed too much leeway earlier, when government oversight was considered "a hindrance more than a help."

Another method that he chose to assert control is decidedly low-tech: printouts of charts, hung from whiteboards on all four walls of a "war room" in the F-35 offices near the Pentagon.

"It looks maybe a little dinosaurlike," he acknowledged, standing near cutout plane shapes tracking the flow of parts into Lockheed's mile-long plant in Fort Worth. "But you know what? It works."

Military officials said the testing had picked up substantially at the Patuxent River Naval Air Station here and other bases, where the planes have already flown near their top speeds of Mach 1.6. Still, the overlap between testing and production remains a serious problem, and the extra cost of refitting planes built while the flight tests are under way could reach $2.4 billion to $3.8 billion, Admiral Venlet said.

Lockheed has already lost profits, earning only $28 million of a possible $87.5 million in award fees for meeting development goals in 2010 and 2011. In tense negotiations over the latest batch, the Pentagon has been demanding that the company shoulder some of the costs of fixing the problems found in the tests.

"It should not take 10, 11, 12 months to negotiate a contract with someone we've been doing business with for 11 years," General Bogdan said.

The general started as Admiral Venlet's deputy in August, and he will succeed him next week. His criticism startled Lockheed officials, because in his last job, overseeing the award of a $35 billion contract for aerial refueling tankers, Boeing gave the Air Force such a good price that analysts think Boeing is subsidizing the early work.

Lockheed argues that the government's estimates of what the F-35s should cost now are too low and that the program was far riskier than the military said it would be. Only 20 to 30 percent of the structural parts ended up in common, though the models will share engines and software. Lockheed officials also noted that commercial plane makers had run into delays with their most innovative planes, Boeing's 787 Dreamliner and Airbus's A350.

Mr. Stevens, the Lockheed chief executive, said military programs bog down in many layers of auditing, a process he described as "sclerosis in the system." In World War II, he said, "We managed to either invent or refine jet propulsion, nuclear weapons, radar, radio communication, electronics in three years and eight months." In that time today, he said, the Pentagon cannot even finish the initial design of a system.

Lockheed is fixing the most glaring problems. A support wall in the fuselage of the Marine version — the only one that can land like a helicopter — was strengthened after it cracked in a test in 2010. The tail-hook on the Navy model was just seven feet behind the landing gear, much closer than on other Navy planes. After the wheels flattened the arresting cable, the cable did not bounce up quickly enough for the hook to grab it. Lockheed is reshaping the hook to try to scoop up the cable.

But the "gorilla in the room," General Bogdan said, is testing and securing the 24 million lines of software code for the plane and its support systems, a mountain of instructions that goes far beyond what has been tried in any plane.

Under the latest plan, Lockheed will be held to about 30 planes in each of the next two years. But the Pentagon will still have bought 365 planes before the flight tests end in 2017.

Two years ago, General Bogdan said, the F-35 program was like an aircraft carrier that "was going to run aground." But if the military and Lockheed can "hold each other accountable," he said, "we've got a shot at getting this done."

ROUGH SKIES AHEAD

With the budget problems at home, Pentagon and Lockheed officials are looking to allies to help pay for the F-35. They have stepped up phone calls and visits, trying to reassure the eight countries that have invested in the program, as well as persuading two others, Israel and Japan, to sign up.

Lockheed needs more foreign orders to realize volume savings and get closer to the Pentagon's targets of $79 million to $106 million a plane, depending on the model. But to get those orders, said Mr. Aboulafia, the Teal Group analyst, Lockheed must be more aggressive in cutting its prices, especially since the allies have their own economic difficulties.

This year, Italy cut its planned order 30 percent. Britain and Australia have delayed decisions on how many F-35s to buy. Lawmakers in Canada and the Netherlands are questioning the costs.

And while Congress continues to support the F-35, the leaders of the Senate Armed Services Committee are concerned that production is now set to ramp up later in this decade just as two other major projects — the refueling tankers and a $55 billion stealth bomber program — will seek financing.

On top of that, the F-35 could be too sophisticated for minor conflicts, and its relatively short flight range could be a problem as the Pentagon changes its view of possible threats. Mark Gunzinger, a retired Air Force colonel who is now an analyst at the Center for Strategic and Budgetary Assessments, said the Pentagon would need to shift money to longer-range planes as China and other countries expanded the reach of missiles capable of destroying American ships and bases.

The Navy is developing a stealthy unmanned fighter that could fly from carriers and go two or three times as far as the F-35. The Air Force is studying concepts for the bomber, which could fly much farther and carry more firepower than the F-35.

Representative Norm Dicks of Washington, the top Democrat on the House defense appropriations subcommittee, said support for the F-35 could also dwindle if lawmakers faced tougher choices between military and domestic programs. "Anything where there are still issues hanging out is going to be vulnerable to some extent," he said.

Pentagon Drops Backup Helmet for F-35 Pilots

BY CHRISTOPHER DREW | OCT. 10, 2013

THE PENTAGON SAID on Thursday that it had decided to stop working on a conventional backup helmet for pilots of the new F-35 fighter jet and stick with a troubled, but improving, higher-tech model.

The advanced helmet is meant to project targeting data onto its visor so pilots can keep track of enemy planes as they swivel their heads to look out the cockpit window.

But the new helmet, being developed by Rockwell Collins and Israel's Elbit Systems, ran into problems, including jittery images, delays in data signals and a green glow that made using its night vision features difficult.

As a result, the military office in charge of developing the jet hired BAE Systems in 2011 to develop a more traditional backup helmet as work continued on the new one.

Pentagon officials said on Thursday that they were now more confident that Rockwell and Elbit could fix the new helmet by making software changes and installing a new camera system. They said they could save $45 million by dropping the backup helmet system. The Pentagon is creating versions of the fighter for the Air Force, Navy and Marines. The program is by far its most expensive, with cost estimates of $391 billion for 2,443 of the jets by the late 2030s.

The overall project also has run into substantial delays and cost overruns with other systems.

Joe DellaVedova, a spokesman for the program, said the Marine Corps would use an early and much more limited version of the new helmets when it started flying the jets in July 2015.

He said Rockwell and Elbit Systems had cut the price of the new helmet by 12 percent, but the full version of it would not be ready until 2017.

The World Awaits the F-35, the Latest in Flying Firepower

BY NICOLA CLARK | JULY 11, 2014

THE BUSINESS BATTLE between Boeing and Airbus traditionally dominates the Farnborough International Airshow. But this weeklong event, which starts on Monday in Hampshire, England, is also a showcase for some of the world's most sophisticated flying weaponry, which perform dazzling displays in the hope of luring prospective government clients.

That includes the expected international air show debut of the F-35, or Joint Strike Fighter. Financed by the United States and Britain, the F-35, built by Lockheed Martin, is one of the world's most ambitious weapons programs, with estimated development costs of around $400 billion.

With government deficits running high, military budgets in the United States and Europe remain constrained by political pressures. And yet, recent political tensions in the Middle East and Asia are bringing security concerns to the fore in those regions, focusing the attention of their cash-rich militaries on a range of new manned and unmanned aerial systems.

At the same time, tensions over Western sanctions against Moscow have led to a smaller-than-usual turnout by Russian manufacturers and the absence of typical crowd-pleasers like the Sukhoi Su-35 fighter from the flyover roster. While no major military orders are expected to emerge from the show, the American industry's presence is expected to be heftier than it was at last year's Paris Air Show, when a deadlock over the United States government's debt ceiling set off billions of dollars in spending cuts and led many American contractors to stay home or send only modest-size delegations.

A number of American-made planes will be presented at Farnborough, including the P-8A Poseidon surveillance plane from Boeing; it was recently deployed to the southern Indian Ocean to search for the missing Malaysia Airlines jet.

But it is the F-35 that is expected to dominate the industry's attention, either by its presence or its absence. An F-35 engine fire on an air base runway in Florida last month prompted the Pentagon last week to temporarily ground its entire training fleet of 97 F-35 fighters. A continuing investigation is expected to force Lockheed to abandon plans to demonstrate the F-35 at another British air show this weekend. But the company said it remained hopeful the plane would still make an appearance at the Farnborough show next week.

The Pentagon has committed to buying more than 2,400 of the single-engine, supersonic planes, which are designed to be almost undetectable by radar. A dozen other American allies — including Australia, Canada, Israel and Japan — have signaled plans to purchase as many as 700 total.

But technical delays and cost overruns have led a number of prospective customers to waver. Britain, which originally said it would buy 138 of the planes, has so far committed to only 48. Meanwhile, debt-laden Italy is considering cutting its order for 90 F-35s by up to half. Last year, the Netherlands reduced its planned purchase to 37 jets, from 85.

The first F-35s are scheduled to be ready for combat service with the United States Marine Corps by the end of next year. But with the plane's cost averaging around $100 million, some analysts say the F-35's export appeal could be limited, especially in smaller countries whose military requirements can be met with cheaper hardware like the Eurofighter Typhoon, Dassault's Rafale or the Saab Gripen.

South Korea and Singapore are among those studying F-35 purchases, while a number of countries in the Persian Gulf have also expressed interest, particularly given their increasing wariness of Iran.

But until now, Washington has prohibited Lockheed from actively marketing the plane to Arab states, in line with United States policy guidelines aimed at preserving Israel's competitive military edge in the region. Typically, American contractors wait about five years before offering similar technology to Israel's neighbors. Israel is expected to receive the first of 19 F-35s it has ordered in 2016, meaning that interested Arab states would not have access to the fighter before early next decade.

"The U.S. makes it extremely difficult for these countries to acquire those aircraft," said Michel Merluzeau, a managing partner of G2 Solutions, an aerospace consultancy in Kirkland, Wash. "So there is a real chance those countries are going to migrate to other platforms."

Air Force Plans Shift to Obtain High-Tech Weapon Systems

BY HELENE COOPER | JULY 30, 2014

WASHINGTON — In an acknowledgment that the military may be pricing itself out of business, the Air Force on Wednesday called for a shift away from big-ticket weapon systems that take decades to develop and a move toward high-technology armaments that can be quickly adapted to meet a range of emerging threats.

An Air Force strategic forecast, looking 20 years into the future and spurred in part by looming budget constraints, also calls for a faster pace, with lower price tags, in developing both airmen and the technology they use, warning that the current way of acquiring warplanes and weapons is too plodding.

The report, described as a "call to action" by Secretary Deborah Lee James of the Air Force, limits itself to how the country's most tech-heavy military service can adapt to looming threats and budget constraints. But it is also a warning to and an admission from the entire Defense Department that with military compensation and retirement costs rising sharply, the country may soon be unable to afford the military it has without making significant changes to the way it does business.

"To boil this down, we have to buy things very differently and develop and employ our people differently," said Maj. Gen. David W. Allvin, one of the authors of the report. "We have to behave more like an innovative 21st-century company."

From 1998 to 2014, annual compensation costs per active-duty service member increased by 76 percent, to $123,000, while the overall defense budget increased by 42 percent — yet, since 2010, the base Defense Department budget, not including spending on the wars in Iraq and Afghanistan, has been declining, according to the Center for Strategic and Budgetary Assessments. So far, the military has dealt with the sharp increase in personnel costs by cutting the number of service members, and has managed to keep expensive weapons acquisition and technology at the same percentage of the overall budget — around 30 percent — as personnel and maintenance and training.

But with the Army, the largest branch in the military, now headed to its lowest personnel numbers since before the World War II buildup, Defense Department officials, particularly in the Army, warn that more cuts could bring increased risks to deployed service members. While the Air Force and Navy, with historic reliance on technology, are widely viewed as more willing to make personnel cuts than their Marine and Army counterparts, even officials in those services say there is a limit to how much more they are willing to reduce personnel.

But a potential gap between good intentions and spending reality remains, and it is unclear how serious the Air Force is about its call to move away from its focus on big, expensive weaponry, in particular advanced fighters and bombers. After all, the report is a long-range forecast that looks to change the culture of weapons development two decades or more down the road, so expensive weapons already in the pipeline remain relatively safe.

Over past decades, similar talk of streamlining the military has crashed into opposition from members of Congress, defense contractors and the military itself, which often work to protect bases, weapons systems and other budget pets. And calls for saving money by adopting new technologies are not new; Donald H. Rumsfeld, a former defense secretary, announced a goal of imposing "transformation" on the military to create a smaller, lighter, more agile — and cheaper — force, but his ideas were forced aside by the terrorist attacks of Sept. 11, 2001, and the wars in Afghanistan and Iraq.

For example, nowhere in the report is there mention of scaling back on the trouble-plagued F-35 jet fighter — in development for 14 years so far — which was temporarily grounded last month after another in a series of problems. Nor is there talk of getting rid the next generation long-range bomber, which the Air Force is working on for around $550 million per plane and which is expected to debut somewhere around the mid-2020s.

"They're still going to buy the Joint Strike Fighter," said Todd Harrison, a senior fellow at the Center for Strategic and Budgetary Assessments, referring to the F-35 warplane. "They're getting squeezed, but they're still going to buy the next generation bomber and the KC-46 tanker" for aerial refueling.

In fact, introducing the report on Wednesday, both Secretary James and Gen. Mark A. Welsh III, the service's chief of staff, made a point of saying that the F-35, the next-generation long-range bomber and the KC-46 refueling tanker are all high-priority items for purchase. General Welsh offered a vigorous defense of the F-35, the world's most expensive weapons project, and called the recent failure of an F-35 engine at a Florida air base a fixable problem.

"The F-35 is the answer, the only answer, that ensures that future fights won't be fair fights," he said. "I'm confident that the program will remain on track."

Officials said Air Force weapons systems that could be targeted in the new shift — the Air Force is calling it "strategic agility" — is the next-generation replacement for the Joint Surveillance Target Attack Radar System, or J-Stars, a surveillance airplane that provides information on ground forces to commanders in the air and on the ground, as well as the replacement training aircraft — called TX — used to train pilots.

Space and information programs could also see their spending cut in this new approach, military analysts said, with a view to building them in a more piecemeal way that would allow for quick adaptation as new technology emerges.

"The notion is, we can't afford the big bang programs anymore, so what if we approached it differently, looking at adding capability in smaller chunks?" said Beth McGrath, a director at Deloitte Consulting and former deputy chief management officer for the Defense Department. "We say, 'This is the big thing we want,' and then we go buy the big thing. But there's a better way to do this."

Air Force officials said they also believed they could incorporate this new system into some existing programs — the service has been retrofitting its aging B-52 bomber fleet for decades to meet changing needs. A senior Air Force official said Wednesday that engineers were looking into whether they could integrate some of the newest advances in aircraft engines, including the latest in propulsion technology for fuel savings, and put them into existing systems, instead of simply starting from scratch all over again with new planes.

General Allvin, who worked on the report, said in an interview that the service also must look for how to make airmen more adaptable to new technology, and seek ways to harness advances underway at American tech giants like Google. He suggested that the Air Force might restructure pension and retirement programs so airmen could still qualify for military retirement benefits even if they spend their careers switching back and forth between the service and high-tech firms in the private sector.

"What if you entered the Air Force knowing you could serve for a few years, then go to work for an innovative tech company, and then return to the Air Force?" he said. "We could enter into partnerships with cutting-edge companies and allow our work force the opportunity of a more flexible retirement system that allows you to do two different jobs and still get to a 20-year retirement. It might take 35 years, but you would get here."

After two costly and exhausting land wars and the fiscal reality of government austerity, the Air Force report could signal similar shifts by the entire military.

Despite Decades of Stealth, Sticking Points Bedevil F-35 Jet

BY CLYDE HABERMAN | JAN. 24, 2016

ONE OF THE EARLIEST stealth weapons on record was a stone used by the young Israelite David to kill the Philistine giant Goliath. In the biblical account, David shunned the conventional armaments of his time: sword, helmet, armor. Instead, he went forth with a slingshot and a few stones, kept undetected in a pouch. As any schoolchild knows, one well-aimed fling was all it took to put Goliath down for good. The big guy never saw it coming.

It is not clear to what extent David tested his weapon before doing battle, but he presumably had experimented. The first Book of Samuel tells how he had earlier struck and killed a lion and a bear that menaced the sheep he tended.

In a sense, not much is different with today's far more sophisticated arsenals; development and testing remain essential. Only the costs and the stakes are considerably higher now, as is made evident in this latest offering from the video documentary producers of Retro Report, who have focused on a supersonic stealth plane called the F-35 Joint Strike Fighter. While still a work in progress, it has already become the most expensive weapons project in military history.

By the time the F-35 program is fully up and running — with an American fleet of more than 2,400 planes planned by the late 2030s — projected total costs will exceed $1 trillion. One billion dollars will be needed just to pay for the highly advanced pilot helmets, running to $400,000 apiece. And though champions of the supersonic F-35 hail it as the ultimate sky fighter for the 21st century, skeptics ask if it is worth all the money and effort, or even if it will prove as effective in its mission as David's little stone was in its day.

To put it mildly, the Joint Strike Fighter is a complex piece of machinery. History suggests that the more intricate a device is, the more ways there are for things to go wrong. Lt. Gen. Christopher C. Bogdan, the Air Force officer in charge of F-35 development, stands firmly by the program, but he acknowledged to Retro Report that the plane's initial design may have been overambitious and thus trouble prone.

Red flags went up even before the Pentagon awarded the contract to Lockheed Martin in October 2001. The Government Accountability Office, Congress's research arm then known as the General Accounting Office, cautioned that assorted technological problems raised the specter of cost overruns, performance failures and production delays. All those fears were borne out. The project is seven years behind schedule, costs have soared, and eyebrows arched higher after a prototype was outmaneuvered by an older F-16 in a mock dogfight early last year.

Lockheed Martin and the F-35's supporters within the military respond that the whole point of the stealth technology is to enable pilots to slip through enemy defenses undetected, fire on ground targets and make a getaway before the other side can figure out what happened. No fuss, no muss — and certainly no dogfight. But, as usual whenever a better mouse comes along, someone is bound to devise a better mousetrap. Improved radar and infrared sensors, some experts say, may make these planes not quite as clandestine as hoped for.

Not that anyone ever claimed stealth engineering was equivalent to an invisibility cloak out of "Harry Potter." "The reality is that there's no such thing as absolute stealth," Gen. Norton A. Schwartz, a former Air Force chief of staff who retired in 2012, told Retro Report. That much was made painfully clear in 1999 when Serbian ground fire brought down an F-117 Nighthawk, an American stealth fighter. It did not appear to be a lucky shot. The plane had been spotted.

The real objective is not invisibility but minimizing a plane's footprint in the sky — its radar cross section — so that it can seem no bigger to monitoring systems than, say, a golf ball. The plane is coated with nonmetallic materials that absorb radar waves. Smooth curves and other design elements can also redirect those waves. Essential features that might be dead giveaways, like the weaponry, are tucked inside the aircraft. Engines are cooled to reduce their thermal signature.

As the video points out, stealth technology entered public consciousness at the start of the 1980s. Perhaps no plane became more instantly recognizable than the B-2 Spirit, a sleek, dark and tail-less bomber that looked like something Batman might have at the ready. The F-35 is the most recent addition to the United States fleet, and it is intended principally to attack targets on the ground, not to engage in air-to-air combat.

It breaks with the past by meeting the requirements of three military branches — the Air Force, Navy and Marines — each of which traditionally developed its own planes. Three in one. Swiss Army knife. Jack-of-all-trades. These are some of the labels attached to the F-35.

As much as 80 percent of its parts are the same for all three services, including engines, fuselage, weapons and supersonic capability. Each branch, however, will have its own variant: a conventional takeoff and landing version for the Air Force, a model that can perform short takeoffs and landings on Navy aircraft carriers, and a helicopter-like design that makes possible the vertical landings desired by the Marines.

Having the services share most of the technology was meant to be a big money saver. But harsh realities intruded, in part because it is complicated, not to mention expensive, to give each branch what it wants. To help defray expenses, the United States has signed up eight other countries as paying partners. But at least one of them, Canada, may be rethinking its commitment. The recently elected prime minister, Justin Trudeau, promised during his campaign to pull out of the program, though he has yet to act on that pledge. A Canadian withdrawal, still not a certainty, would increase the costs for everyone else.

Budgetary worries are such that Senator John McCain, Republican of Arizona and chairman of the Senate Armed Services Committee, has dismissed the plan for 2,400 planes as unrealistic. "The number they are now quoting — there's just not going to be that many," Mr. McCain said in late October.

For others, there is also the fact that the F-35, as an all-purpose workhorse, is intended to replace a flock of warplanes that are aging but have proved worthy, including the F-16, the A-10 attack plane and the AV-8B Harrier. The plan to retire the A-10 in particular is being delayed for at least a year, in good measure because of resistance in Congress.

Others have their own doubts about putting the old-timers out to pasture. They include War Is Boring, a website that often casts a jaundiced eye on military decisions. Skeptical about the F-35's capabilities, it has suggested that it is a mistake for the Pentagon to bet pretty much everything on this one fighter.

Even David understood that it would be unwise to take on Goliath with only one projectile in his arsenal. The Bible says he first picked out five smooth stones from a brook. Plainly, he understood the importance of having a backup system.

Trump's Push to Cut Jet Costs Hits a Nerve, but His Demands Face Limitations

BY CHRISTOPHER DREW | DEC. 23, 2016

AFTER MEETING WITH Lockheed Martin's chief executive on Wednesday about lowering the cost of its new F-35 fighter jet, President-elect Donald J. Trump expressed confidence that Pentagon officials standing with him were "good negotiators" and could "get it done beautifully."

Then, on Thursday, he gave the talks another jolt, posting on Twitter that he had asked Lockheed's rival, Boeing, for a price quote on the most comparable version of its older F/A-18 Super Hornet.

Based on the tremendous cost and cost overruns of the Lockheed Martin F-35, I have asked Boeing to price-out a comparable F-18 Super Hornet!

— Donald J. Trump (@realDonaldTrump) Dec. 22, 2016

And on Friday, Lockheed's chief, Marillyn Hewson, made clear she got the message.

"I had a very good conversation with President-elect Trump this afternoon and assured him that I've heard his message loud and clear about reducing the cost of the F-35," she said. "I gave him my personal commitment to drive the cost down aggressively."

Besides the drama of his personal intervention, Mr. Trump had made it clear that he would like to squeeze Lockheed for a better deal and might try to shift some of the fighter business to Boeing if he does not get it. Rarely have presidents taken such negotiations into their own hands, and his post — along with an earlier one rapping Boeing over the cost of a new Air Force One — sent shock waves through the military industry, which is bracing for volatile dealings with Mr.

Boeing's F-18 Super Hornet jet. Defense contractors are bracing for volatile dealings with Donald J. Trump over projects.

Trump over projects to update nuclear weapons and build new bombers and missile submarines.

So far, Lockheed Martin is the biggest target. It depends on the F-35 for nearly a quarter of its revenues, and Mr. Trump has not indicated whether he just wants a better price for each plane or might scale back the program. At an estimated $400 billion for 2,443 planes — being built in different versions for the Air Force, the Marines and the Navy — the high-tech fighter is by far the largest weapons project, and it is long overdue.

"As in the business world, he's laying out this combative posture," said Gordon Adams, who oversaw military budgets in the Clinton White House. "He's doing it like a real estate deal. It's amazing."

But while taxpayers want to see the government clamp down on arms costs, Mr. Adams added, "there is not an Option B" with some of these programs, "only an Option A, and you've got to make it work."

Others said that even if Mr. Trump persuaded Lockheed to lower its price a bit, he could end up ratifying a shift that had already been underway, with the Navy buying more of Boeing's Super Hornets along with the F-35s.

"He's coming to it a little late in the game," said Richard L. Aboulafia, an aviation analyst at the Teal Group in Fairfax, Va. "The Navy has been buying the Super Hornet along with the F-35 for several years, and they will be taking even more Super Hornets, and he says something and makes it look like he is in charge."

For the Navy, the planes complement each other but are not interchangeable, and it would be impossible for the Super Hornets to supplant more than a fraction of the F-35s that the Pentagon wants.

Mr. Trump has not commented beyond his Twitter message, and his transition team did not respond on Friday to a request for comment on his plans for the F-35 program.

The Air Force and the Marines have no interest in buying Super Hornets, and most experts say that the Navy still needs to buy F-35s for its most sensitive missions. The F-35s are designed with radar-evading stealth protection, and the Super Hornets, which were designed in the 1990s, have only limited stealth attributes.

So while the Super Hornets have been busy conducting bombing runs against the Islamic State in Iraq and Syria, the F-35 would be the Navy's best choice for trying to sneak into China early in a larger war to knock out antiaircraft installations. Asked if he would rather fly an F-35 than a Super Hornet on that type of mission, Mr. Aboulafia said, "Oh, God, yes."

The F-35 was conceived as the Pentagon's silver bullet in the sky — a state-of-the art aircraft that could be adapted to the three branches of the military, with advances that would easily overcome the defenses of most foes. The radar-evading jets would not only dodge sophisticated antiaircraft missiles, but they would also give pilots a better picture of enemy threats while enabling 11 allied countries, which also want the planes, to fight more closely with American forces.

But the ambitious aircraft instead illustrates how the Pentagon can let huge and complex programs veer out of control and then struggle to rein them in. The program nearly doubled in cost from 2001 to 2010 as Lockheed and the military's own bureaucracy failed to deliver on the most basic promise of a three-in-one jet that would save taxpayers money and be produced speedily.

The Pentagon temporarily slowed purchases of the jets several years ago to stabilize the program, and Lockheed has now built 204 of them. Pentagon officials said recently that the program would need an extra $500 million but that it remained roughly on a revised schedule.

In November, the Pentagon imposed a price cut on the latest batch of the planes after Lockheed refused to agree to terms. The various versions of the F-35 range in cost from about $102 million to $132 million apiece, and Lockheed thinks it can lower that to $80 million to $85 million by 2019. The Super Hornets typically sell for $60 million to $70 million.

The Marines said their version of the F-35, which flies like a jet but can take off and land almost vertically like a helicopter, was ready for initial operations last year, and the Air Force began limited operations with its version in August. The Navy plans to wait until 2018, when the full war-fighting software is ready, to put planes into service.

Some Pentagon officials remain skeptical that the millions of lines of software code can be completed on time, and outside analysts say that the purchases could eventually be trimmed to 1,200 to 1,500 planes. Right now, the Air Force plans to buy 1,763 of the planes and the Marines and the Navy 680.

Still, most analysts say it would be hard to stop the program now. The Pentagon has already spent $100 billion on it, and there would be diplomatic fallout with other countries that have invested in the program. Cuts could also encounter resistance in Congress because Lockheed has spread subcontractors — and jobs — through nearly every state.

Boeing is in a much better position in dealing with Mr. Trump's demands to cut costs on the Air Force One project, analysts said. That program is in an early phase, and Boeing has received only $170 million in study contracts.

Mr. Trump has claimed that it would cost $4 billion to buy two 747-8's and develop antimissile and other sophisticated communications and defensive gear, but the Pentagon's own estimate is about $3 billion.

Boeing's chief executive, Dennis A. Muilenburg, also met with Mr. Trump on Wednesday and said afterward that he had given Mr. Trump "my personal commitment" to hold costs down.

Boeing has said it did not expect to earn much on the planes. It also would like to win Mr. Trump's support for a plan to sell $16.6 billion in commercial aircraft to Iran and other measures to help its export sales.

Glossary

acquisition The act of getting or buying something.

arsenal A stockpile of weapons ready for use.

audit An inspection of a system, often by a person or group outside the system.

bureaucracy Complicated administrative procedures that involve decisions made by many state officials.

comptroller An official who performs audits.

contingency A plan for a future event that cannot be predicted but is possible.

deficit A shortfall or debt; an amount spent that exceeds the amount one brings in. Often used in relation to trade (a country's imports exceed their exports) or to budgets (spending is greater than income).

deficit hawk A government official whose policies favor decreasing the budget deficit or limiting government spending to the amount the government takes in via taxes.

deter To incentivize someone not to do something; the concept is important in nuclear balance in which it would not be beneficial for either side to use its nuclear weapons.

G.A.O. (U.S. Government Accountability Office) Group of analysts and economists who write reports for Congress.

inflation The increase in prices and decline in value of money.

infrastructure The foundation, physical and logical, on which a system is made possible; e.g., roads, sewers and electrical grids make modern societies possible.

isolationism The strategy of decreasing foreign entanglements, e.g., producing one's own energy rather than buying it from another country or not intervening in wars that occur in another country.

lobbyist A representative of an industry or group whose job it is to persuade different government agencies to pass rules or laws that help the private interests they represent.

monopoly Having exclusive control over a commodity or service.

oversight Watching over or holding some group of actors accountable for making sound decisions.

Pentagon Headquarters for the U.S. Department of Defense, just outside of Washington, D.C.

profligacy Wasteful behavior.

proliferation Increasing the number of; often used to refer to building more weapons, e.g., "nuclear proliferation."

sabotage Undermining, destroying or obstructing something, usually to gain some advantage.

subcommittee A committee made up of members of a larger committee, e.g., in Congress.

Media Literacy Terms

"Media literacy" refers to the ability to access, understand, critically assess and create media. The following terms are important components of media literacy, and they will help you critically engage with the articles in this title.

angle The aspect of a news story that a journalist focuses on and develops.

attribution The method by which a source is identified or by which facts and information are assigned to the person who provided them.

balance Principle of journalism that both perspectives of an argument should be presented in a fair way.

column A type of story that is a regular feature, often on a recurring topic, written by the same journalist, generally known as a columnist.

commentary A type of story that is an expression of opinion on recent events by a journalist generally known as a commentator.

credibility The quality of being trustworthy and believable, said of a journalistic source.

editorial Article of opinion or interpretation.

fake news A fictional or made-up story presented in the style of a legitimate news story, intended to deceive readers; also commonly used to criticize legitimate news because of its perspective or unfavorable coverage of a subject.

feature story Article designed to entertain as well as to inform.

human interest story A type of story that focuses on individuals and how events or issues affect their lives, generally offering a sense of relatability to the reader.

impartiality Principle of journalism that a story should not reflect a journalist's bias and should contain balance.

intention The motive or reason behind something, such as the publication of a news story.

interview story A type of story in which the facts are gathered primarily by interviewing another person or persons.

motive The reason behind something, such as the publication of a news story or a source's perspective on an issue.

news story An article or style of expository writing that reports news, generally in a straightforward fashion and without editorial comment.

op-ed An opinion piece that reflects a prominent individual's opinion on a topic of interest.

paraphrase The summary of an individual's words, with attribution, rather than a direct quotation of their exact words.

quotation The use of an individual's exact words indicated by the use of quotation marks and proper attribution.

reliability The quality of being dependable and accurate, said of a journalistic source.

source The origin of the information reported in journalism.

style A distinctive use of language in writing or speech; also a news or publishing organization's rules for consistent use of language with regard to spelling, punctuation, typography and capitalization, usually regimented by a house style guide.

tone A manner of expression in writing or speech.

Media Literacy Questions

1. Identify the various sources cited in the article "Costliest Jet, Years in Making, Sees the Enemy: Budget Cuts" (on page 185). How does Christopher Drew attribute information to each of these sources in his article? How effective are Drew's attributions in helping the reader identify his sources?

2. What type of story is "Broad Ripples of Iraq War in Budgets of 2 Agencies" (on page 78)? Can you identify another article in this collection that is the same type of story? What elements helped you come to your conclusion?

3. The article "Reigning In Soldiers of Fortune" (on page 131) is an example of an op-ed. Identify how Sean Mcfate's attitude and tone help convey his opinion on the topic.

4. Does "Audit of Pentagon Spending Finds $70 Billion in Waste" (on page 178) use multiple sources? What are the strengths of using multiple sources in a journalistic piece? What are the weaknesses of relying heavily on only one or a few sources?

5. Do Declan Walsh and Eric Schmitt demonstrate the journalistic principle of impartiality in their article "Arms Sales to Saudis Leave American Fingerprints on Yemen's Carnage" (on page 95)? If so, how did they do so? If not, what could they have included to make their article more impartial?

6. What is the intention of the article "Dayton Counting on Military" (on page 114)? How effectively does it achieve its intended purpose?

7. Identify each of the sources in "As Wars End, a Rush to Grab Dollars Spent on the Border" (on page 88) as a primary source or a secondary source. Evaluate the reliability and credibility of each source. How does your evaluation of each source change your perspective on this article?

8. The article "These Toilet Seat Lids Aren't Gold-Plated, but They Cost $14,000" (on page 59) is an example of an op-ed. Identify how Charles Grassley's attitude and tone help convey his opinion on the topic.

9. In "$296 Billion in Overruns in U.S. Weapons Programs" (on page 26), Christopher Drew paraphrases information from a G.A.O. audit report. What are the strengths of the use of a paraphrase as opposed to a direct quote? What are the weaknesses?

10. Compare the headlines of "The Pentagon Doesn't Know Where Its Money Goes" (on page 54) and "These Toilet Seat Lids Aren't Gold-Plated, but They Cost $14,000" (on page 59). Which is a more compelling headline, and why? How could the less compelling headline be changed to better draw the reader's interest?

11. "Military Is Asked to March to a Less Expensive Tune" (on page 40) features photographs. What do these photographs add to the article?

Citations

All citations in this list are formatted according to the Modern Language Association's (MLA) style guide.

BOOK CITATION

THE NEW YORK TIMES EDITORIAL STAFF. *Military Spending.* New York: New York Times Educational Publishing, 2020.

ONLINE ARTICLE CITATIONS

BUMILLER, ELISABETH. "Costly Aircraft Suggests Cuts Won't Be Easy." *The New York Times*, 19 Nov. 2011, https://www.nytimes.com/2011/11/20/us /costly-osprey-symbol-of-fight-to-cut-pentagon.html.

BUMILLER, ELISABETH, AND THOM SHANKER. "Panetta to Offer Strategy for Cutting Military Budget." *The New York Times*, 2 Jan. 2012, https://www .nytimes.com/2012/01/03/us/pentagon-to-present-vision-of-reduced -military.html.

CLARK, NICOLA. "The World Awaits the F-35, the Latest in Flying Firepower." *The New York Times*, 20 Dec. 2017, https://www.nytimes.com/2014/07/12 /business/the-world-awaits-the-f-35-the-latest-in-flying-firepower.html.

CLOUD, DAVID S., AND JOEL BRINKLEY. "Broad Ripples of Iraq War in Budgets of 2 Agencies." *The New York Times*, 7 Feb. 2006, https://www.nytimes .com/2006/02/07/politics/broad-ripples-of-iraq-war-in-budgets-of-2 -agencies.html.

COOPER, HELENE. "Air Force Plans Shift to Obtain High-Tech Weapon Systems." *The New York Times*, 20 Dec. 2017, https://www.nytimes.com /2014/07/31/us/politics/air-force-calls-for-cheaper-quicker-weapons -development.html.

COOPER, HELENE, AND PETER BAKER. "Critics Assail Cuts in Foreign Spending as Trump Moves to Boost Military." *The New York Times*, 27 Feb. 2017, https://www.nytimes.com/2017/02/27/us/politics/trump-foreign -military-spending-cuts-criticism.html.

DREW, CHRISTOPHER. "Audit of Pentagon Spending Finds $70 Billion in Waste." *The New York Times*, 29 Mar. 2011, https://www.nytimes.com/2011/03/30 /business/30military.html.

DREW, CHRISTOPHER. "Costliest Jet, Years in Making, Sees the Enemy: Budget Cuts." *The New York Times*, 28 Nov. 2012, https://www.nytimes.com /2012/11/29/us/in-federal-budget-cutting-f-35-fighter-jet-is-at-risk.html.

DREW, CHRISTOPHER. "Fear of Lost Jobs Is Hurdle to Reining In Defense Contracts." *The New York Times*, 8 Mar. 2009, https://www.nytimes .com/2009/03/09/us/politics/09defense.html.

DREW, CHRISTOPHER. "Military Costs Under Review in Bid to Trim Waste." *The New York Times*, 27 June 2010, https://www.nytimes.com/2010/06/28 /business/28contracts.html.

DREW, CHRISTOPHER. "Military Expects More Shopping Money, If Not All Trump Seeks." *The New York Times*, 22 Dec. 2017, https://www.nytimes .com/2017/03/02/business/trump-pentagon-budget.html.

DREW, CHRISTOPHER. "Pentagon Drops Backup Helmet for F-35 Pilots." *The New York Times*, 19 Oct. 2018, https://www.nytimes.com/2013/10/11 /business/pentagon-drops-backup-helmet-for-f-35-pilots.html.

DREW, CHRISTOPHER. "Trump's Push to Cut Jet Costs Hits a Nerve, but His Demands Face Limitations." *The New York Times*, 22 Dec. 2017, https://www .nytimes.com/2016/12/23/business/trump-lockheed-boeing-jet-costs.html.

DREW, CHRISTOPHER. "$296 Billion in Overruns in U.S. Weapons Programs." *The New York Times*, 30 Mar. 2009, https://www.nytimes.com/2009/03/31 /business/31defense.html.

GANSLER, JACQUES S. "To Save on Defense, Hire Rivals." *The New York Times*, 20 Dec. 2017, https://www.nytimes.com/2014/02/27/opinion/to-save-on -defense-hire-rivals.html.

GELB, LESLIE H. "Arms Talks: A Signal and a Beginning." *The New York Times*, 9 Jan. 1985, https://www.nytimes.com/1985/01/09/world/arms-talks-a -signal-and-a-beginning.html.

GRASSLEY, CHARLES. "These Toilet Seat Lids Aren't Gold-Plated, but They Cost $14,000." *The New York Times*, 20 Dec. 2018, https://www.nytimes .com/2018/12/19/opinion/pentagon-budget-military-spending-waste.html.

HABERMAN, CLYDE. "Despite Decades of Stealth, Sticking Points Bedevil F-35 Jet." *The New York Times*, 21 Dec. 2017, https://www.nytimes.com /2016/01/25/us/despite-decades-of-stealth-sticking-points-bedevil -f-35-jet.html.

KELLER, BILL. "Cut the Military Budget? Oh, Sure." *The New York Times*,
14 Jan. 1985, https://www.nytimes.com/1985/01/14/us/congress-cut-the
-military-budget-oh-sure.html.

KRAUSS, CLIFFORD. "Linking Arms Cuts to Taxes." *The New York Times*, 7 Jan.
1992, https://www.nytimes.com/1992/01/07/us/linking-arms-cuts-to-taxes
.html.

LIPTON, ERIC. "As Wars End, a Rush to Grab Dollars Spent on the Border."
The New York Times, 19 Oct. 2018, https://www.nytimes.com/2013/06/07
/us/us-military-firms-eye-border-security-contracts.html.

MCDOWELL, EDWIN. "Arms Makers Are the Top Beneficiaries; A Banner
Budget for Arms Makers." *The New York Times*, 20 Jan. 1980, https://
www.nytimes.com/1980/01/20/archives/arms-makers-are-the-top
-beneficiaries-a-banner-budget-for-arms.html.

MCFATE, SEAN. "Reining In Soldiers of Fortune." *The New York Times*, 21 Dec.
2017, https://www.nytimes.com/2015/04/18/opinion/reining-in-soldiers-of
-fortune.html.

MCINNIS, DOUG. "Dayton Counting on Military." *The New York Times*,
14 Jan. 1985, https://www.nytimes.com/1985/01/14/business/dayton
-counting-on-military.html.

METZ, ROBERT. "Defense Stocks Go on Offensive." *The New York Times*,
8 Jan. 1980, https://www.nytimes.com/1980/01/08/archives/market
-place-defense-stocks-go-on-offensive.html.

THE NEW YORK TIMES. "A Better, Not Bigger, Military Budget." *The New York
Times*, 19 Jan. 2018, https://www.nytimes.com/2016/02/29/opinion/a
-better-not-bigger-military-budget.html.

THE NEW YORK TIMES. "A Better, Not Fatter, Defense Budget." *The New York
Times*, 21 Dec. 2017, https://www.nytimes.com/2016/05/09/opinion/a
-better-not-fatter-defense-budget.html.

THE NEW YORK TIMES. "Blackwater's Rich Contracts." *The New York Times*,
3 Oct. 2007, https://www.nytimes.com/2007/10/03/opinion/03wed2.html.

THE NEW YORK TIMES. "Modernizing the Military, With a Technological
Edge." *The New York Times*, 6 Feb. 2012, https://www.nytimes.com
/2012/02/07/opinion/modernizing-the-military-with-a-technological
-edge.html.

THE NEW YORK TIMES. "National Defense: Against What?" *The New York
Times*, 8 Jan. 1990, https://timesmachine.nytimes.com/timesmachine
/1990/01/08/996090.html.

THE NEW YORK TIMES. "New Strategy, Old Pentagon Budget." *The New York Times*, 29 Jan. 2012, https://www.nytimes.com/2012/01/30/opinion /new-strategy-old-pentagon-budget.html.

THE NEW YORK TIMES. "The Pentagon Doesn't Know Where Its Money Goes." *The New York Times*, 7 Dec. 2018, https://www.nytimes.com/2018/12/01 /opinion/sunday/pentagon-spending-audit-failed.html.

THE NEW YORK TIMES. "The Pentagon Is Not a Sacred Cow." *The New York Times*, 14 Dec. 2017, https://www.nytimes.com/2017/12/13/opinion /military-spending-pentagon.html.

THE NEW YORK TIMES. "Pentagon Profligacy." *The New York Times*, 9 Jan. 1970, https://www.nytimes.com/1970/01/09/archives/pentagon-profligacy.html.

THE NEW YORK TIMES. "Senator Blames Congress for High Cost of Military." *The New York Times*, 11 Jan. 1985, https://www.nytimes.com/1985/01/11/us /senator-blames-congress-for-high-cost-of-military.html.

THE NEW YORK TIMES. "Two Very Troubled Fighter Jets." *The New York Times*, 14 July 2012, https://www.nytimes.com/2012/07/15/opinion /sunday/two-very-troubled-fighter-jets.html.

PHILIPPS, DAVE. "Military Is Asked to March to a Less Expensive Tune." *The New York Times*, 21 Dec. 2017, https://www.nytimes.com/2016/07/02/us /military-bands-budget.html.

RISEN, JAMES, AND MARK MAZZETTI. "30 False Fronts Won Contracts for Blackwater." *The New York Times*, 3 Sept. 2010, https://www.nytimes .com/2010/09/04/world/middleeast/04blackwater.html.

SANGER, DAVID E. "Budget Documents Detail Extent of U.S. Cyberoperations." *The New York Times*, 19 Oct. 2018, https://www.nytimes.com/2013/09/01 /world/americas/documents-detail-cyberoperations-by-us.html.

SANGER, DAVID E., AND THOM SHANKER. "Cuts Give Obama Path to Create Leaner Military." *The New York Times*, 19 Oct. 2018, https://www.nytimes .com/2013/03/11/us/politics/mandatory-cuts-could-open-path-to-deeper -defense-trims.html.

SATARIANO, ADAM. "Will There Be a Ban on Killer Robots?" *The New York Times*, 20 Oct. 2018, https://www.nytimes.com/2018/10/19/technology /artificial-intelligence-weapons.html.

SCHMITT, ERIC, AND THOM SHANKER. "U.S. Seeks $3 Billion for Pakistani Military." *The New York Times*, 2 Apr. 2009, https://www.nytimes .com/2009/04/03/washington/03military.html.

SHANKER, THOM. "Defense Chief Ends Probation Status of Marine Warplane." *The New York Times*, 20 Jan. 2012, https://www.nytimes.com/2012/01/21 /us/panetta-ends-probation-of-marines-f-35-fighter-jet.html.

SHANKER, THOM. "Pentagon Tries to Counter Low-Cost but Potent Weapons." *The New York Times*, 9 Jan. 2012, https://www.nytimes .com/2012/01/10/world/pentagon-tries-to-counter-low-cost-but -potent-weapons.html.

SHANKER, THOM. "Proposed Military Spending Is Highest Since WWII." *The New York Times*, 4 Feb. 2008, https://www.nytimes.com/2008/02/04 /washington/04military.html.

UCHITELLE, LOUIS. "The U.S. Still Leans on the Military-Industrial Complex." *The New York Times*, 22 Sept. 2017, https://www.nytimes.com/2017/09/22 /business/economy/military-industrial-complex.html.

WALSH, DECLAN, AND ERIC SCHMITT. "Arms Sales to Saudis Leave American Fingerprints on Yemen's Carnage." *The New York Times*, 26 Dec. 2018, https://www.nytimes.com/2018/12/25/world/middleeast/yemen-us -saudi-civilian-war.html.

WAYNE, LESLIE. "Painting a Rosy Picture of a Costly Fighter Jet." *The New York Times*, 22 June 2007, https://www.nytimes.com/2007/06/22 /business/22strike.html.

WAYNE, LESLIE. "Pentagon Struggles With Cost Overruns and Delays." *The New York Times*, 11 July 2006, https://www.nytimes.com/2006/07/11 /business/11overruns.html.

WEINER, TIM. "Satellite System for the Pentagon Brings Questions." *The New York Times*, 17 Jan. 1994, https://www.nytimes.com/1994/01/17/us /satellite-system-for-the-pentagon-brings-questions.html.

Index

A

Aboulafia, Richard L., 31, 32, 123, 189, 193, 208

acquisitions, 20, 116, 118, 156, 183, 184, 188, 190, 199

Adams, Gordon, 36, 50, 119, 138, 207

Afghanistan, 22, 30, 34, 52, 57, 58, 78, 86–87, 88, 108, 109, 128, 132, 166

Afghanistan War, 29, 36–37, 79, 81, 82, 84, 118, 137, 139, 141–142, 143, 158, 160–161, 164, 185, 187, 190, 198, 199

Airbus Group, 155, 192, 195

aircraft carriers, 33, 46, 121, 138, 145, 148, 150, 176, 182, 187, 192, 193, 204

Air Force One, 47, 206, 209

arsenals
nuclear, 38, 53, 58, 73, 137, 158, 162, 163
weapons, 40, 66, 142, 151, 202, 205

artificial intelligence, 49, 168–169

audits, 10, 19, 26, 53, 54–58, 61–63, 78, 86, 90, 92, 126, 178–179, 192

B

ballistic missiles, 48, 67, 105, 108, 111, 144, 148

Blackwater, 125–126, 127–130, 131, 133

Boeing Corporation, 23, 32, 33, 47, 91–93, 102–103, 104, 107, 110, 111, 155, 167, 170, 189, 191, 192, 195, 206, 208, 209–210

border patrol systems, 91–92

Budget Control Act (2011), 49, 183

budget cuts, 10, 35, 40, 88–89, 138, 147, 185

bureaucracy, 18, 28, 55, 57, 58, 187, 209

Bush, George W., 20, 21, 31, 32, 81, 82, 88, 119, 125, 126, 135, 136, 150, 188

C

Carter, Ashton B., 28, 29, 37

Carter, Jimmy, 105, 106, 108, 109–110, 111, 112

Cato Institute, 141, 157

Center for a New American Security, 139, 141

Center for Strategic and Budgetary Assessments (C.S.B.A.), 83, 140, 141, 187, 193, 198, 200

Center for Strategic and International Studies (C.S.I.S.), 48, 53, 144, 156, 162, 164

Central Intelligence Agency (C.I.A.), 127–130, 131

Cheney, Dick, 31, 32, 33, 125, 134, 135–136

China, 48, 49, 51, 56, 58, 109, 121, 138, 141, 143, 144–145, 150, 151, 152, 157, 160, 188, 193, 208

Chrysler Corporation, 69, 112, 114

Clinton, William J., 36, 50, 119, 138, 156, 188, 207

Cold War, 36, 52, 73, 75, 76, 119, 121, 138, 156, 165

cyber technology, 35, 49, 143, 144, 147, 151–153, 168

D

defense
budgets, 11, 18, 26, 36, 43, 49, 51, 83, 108–110, 112, 136, 139–140, 157, 160, 162, 164, 198
contracts, 8, 11, 26, 58, 94, 109, 112, 116, 118, 120, 170, 184, 199

Demisch, Wolfgang H., 105–106, 109

DeVos, Betsy, 125

drones, 35, 47, 88, 90, 129, 147, 151, 168, 170

F

F-16 aircraft, 23–24, 39, 113, 115, 141, 155, 174, 203, 205

F-22 aircraft, 23–24, 27, 119, 120, 145, 183, 184, 189

This book is current up until the time of printing. For the most up-to-date reporting, visit www.nytimes.com.